wedding

INVITATIONS, ANNOUNCEMENTS, PLACE CARDS, *and* MORE

ROCKPORT

wedding

INVITATIONS, ANNOUNCEMENTS, PLACE CARDS, *and* MORE

GLOUCESTER MASSACHUSETTS

ROCKPORT PUBLISHERS

A Bride's Guide to Simple Calligraphy

Bette Matthews

First published in the United States of America by
Rockport Publishers, Inc.
33 Commercial Street
Gloucester, Massachusetts 01930-5089
Telephone: (978) 282-9590
Facsimile: (978) 283-2742
www.rockpub.com

ISBN 1-56496-808-1

10 9 8 7 6 5 4 3 2 1

Design: Leeann Leftwich

Cover Image: Kevin Thomas

All other photography by
Brian Piper Photography,
West Chester, Pennsylvania.

Layout: SYP Design & Production, Inc.

Printed in China.

In a redwood grove
under a blue skye
Cyndi Chambers
and
Dave Crook
will exchange
marriage vows

Please grace us
with your presence

Sunday, June 16, 1
at 1:30 p.m.

Boulder Cr
Scout Reserva
14586 Bear Cree
Boulder Cr
Califo

Reception
fol

page 32

page 45

page 62

contents

page 82

page 92

page 96

THE CALLIGRAPHIC WEDDING

You've dreamed about this day your entire life. And as you move further and further into the planning process of your wedding, each and every detail seems to grow in importance. Small elements combine to create a full-bodied effect.

The written word has great prominence in wedding festivities. It may be in an obvious capacity, such as invitations, place cards, or menus. Or it may be something less noticeable, such as a favor tag, the name on a guest book, or a handwritten note on a gift basket sent to a guest's hotel room. The opportunities for beautiful lettering are vast. Calligraphy can enhance your writing at its core.

This book provides a basic introduction to calligraphy and some of the multitudes of lettering styles—some simple, others more complex. The instructional opening chapter offers an overview of tools, materials, and technique. The chapters that follow are divided into overall styles: Classic, Elegant, Romantic, Modern, and Artistic. These divisions are purely subjective, so don't feel as if you have to confine your imagination. With a little thought or with minor changes, your alphabet of choice can be translated to any project in the book. Calligraphy is versatile and transcends any classifications we impose upon it.

The projects in this book incorporate a full range of wedding concerns, from engagement to postwedding activities. Invitations, envelopes, and place cards are the most obvious items with which calligraphy is typically used. There are also ideas for gift tags, guest books to record good wishes, programs, and more. The quality of your finished product will be affected by the quality of your materials, so choose fine papers, ribbons, and flowers for these projects, and you won't be disappointed.

The last section of the book is the gallery. This is a showcase of professional work from experienced calligraphers offered to inspire you. Each of these pieces is created by an artist who learned the craft one step at a time, just as you are about to do.

Practice, relax, and enjoy the learning process. Above all, let your own character, your own vision, and your own penmanship shine on the page. Don't strive for perfection; strive for personality.

basic calligrahy
GETTING STARTED

Calligraphy, which literally means "beautiful writing," is the marriage of pen and ink and paper, and in this case, three is *not* a crowd. Finding a comfortable working position, understanding the alphabets, and some basic practice techniques all add up to your first steps toward creating your own calligraphy. In addition, when learning any new craft, it is helpful to understand the tools and materials used to create the work. Outlined in this chapter are some basic techniques, tools, and know-how that will get you started writing beautifully.

YOUR WORK AREA

Sit in an armless chair that supports your lower back and allows for some movement and position shifting to avoid stiffness. Sit up straight, with both feet squarely on the floor. Your work surface should be free of debris and at a height that allows you to write comfortably without reaching or hunching. Place a glare-free lamp on your left if you are right-handed and on the right if you are left-handed, so that your arm and hand do not create shadows on your page.

Although it is possible to work on a flat surface, it is more likely to restrict your arm. A drawing board can be tilted to allow you to work without leaning or hunching, and enables you to see your entire page easily. The board should be at least 26" to 30" (66 cm to 76 cm) wide and 20" to 24" (51 cm to 61 cm) high, and the working angle should be between 30 and 45 degrees. It should be smooth—your pen will catch in any dents or scratches. Angled boards are also available with a Plexiglass™ surface, which, when lit from behind, doubles as a light box.

EQUIPMENT

A light box often eliminates the need for drawing penciled guidelines onto your work. A guide sheet or template is placed on the light box and the working paper is placed on top. The light from the box allows the markings on the lower sheet to be seen through the top sheet. Rules can be followed without drawing them on your final paper, and letterspacing from the template can be followed in calligraphic form.

It is important to align your work so that it is perfectly square with the measurements of the board. The T-square allows you to do this easily by resting on your board and creating a 90-degree angle to draw horizontal, parallel rules. A metal T-square also makes for an excellent cutting edge. Mark all your measurements carefully using a good ruler.

The computer, with accompanying scanner and printer, is a valuable tool. A word-processing program will allow you to do basic layouts. For more refined controls, purchase a page layout program or an image-editing program.

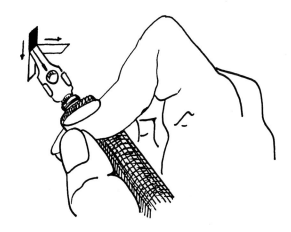

figure 1

figure 2

Copperplate scripts are executed by putting pressure on a flexible nib. A pen can make a swell only as large as the flexibility of the nib will permit. An oblique pen nib is shown here.

swells : begin and end with a hairline

shades : have a hairline at one end and a squared-off end at the other end

connectives : are hairlines that join the letters

figure 2

ILLUSTRATIONS/CALLIGRAPHY BY SUSAN L. RAMSEY

PENS, MARKERS, AND BRUSHES

Many manufacturers make calligraphy pens, and each carries nibs (pen tips) in various sizes, plus penholders to fit their nibs. There is no standard for numbering or naming the nibs; each manufacturer has its own method of identification. Compare the width of the nib to the size of the letters you wish to create. Buy several nibs of different widths so you can alter the shape and size of your letters. Some pens have a built-in reservoir to hold the ink; for others the reservoir slips on.

Broad-Edged Pen. The broad-edged pen *(figure 1)* creates thick and thin lines without pressure, based on the motion of the pen and the angle that the nib is held in relation to the paper. It draws a wide line when moved across the page from top to bottom or from left to right. When moved diagonally, the pen's chiseled edge forms a thin, hairline rule.

Fine-Tipped Pen. The fine-tipped pen *(figure 2)*, also called the pointed pen or crow-quill, has a pointed nib that is used to create the Copperplate scripts on pages 58–59. The thick and thin lines of these alphabets are created by putting pressure on the nib so that more ink flows to the paper. This nib must be sturdy and flexible at the same time, so it can create fine hairlines and thicker swells that define these script alphabets.

Fountain Pens. Fountain pens can be purchased with one nib or in sets with several interchangeable nibs. They are good for the beginner because they have ink cartridges that supply a steady flow of ink to the pen nib, eliminating the need to dip or refill the tip. They usually don't produce as fine or crisp a line as a dip pen. Waterproof or permanent ink will clog a fountain pen.

Pen nibs are sometimes prepackaged with a holder made of wood or plastic, but both are also sold independently. Be sure that the size of your pen nib will fit in the holder—the size and curvature of the base should match. Find one that feels comfortable in your hand.

The elbow pen holder, or oblique holder, for Copperplate scripts has a metal sleeve attached to the grip that holds the fine-tipped nib at a sharp angle, making it easier to maintain the steep angle of the pen point as you work.

Calligraphy markers are used by both beginners and experienced calligraphers. Ranging from extra-fine tips to broad, chiseled calligraphy tips, they are handy for many projects that don't require an extremely crisp or refined line. Paint pens, gel pens, and metallic markers are terrific for adding color and sparkle to your work.

An assortment of small brushes with rounded and pointed tips is necessary for adding watercolor flowers and occasionally filling in a large letter. Also, a small, number-three brush with a rounded tip is useful for filling an ink reservoir. The brush is dipped in ink, which is carefully transferred to the reservoir. This method offers more control over the amount of ink loaded into the reservoir than dipping the pen in an inkwell.

INK AND PAINT

Nonwaterproof ink is widely used for projects that don't require permanence. It has a light, thin consistency that flows well in a calligraphy pen. It is the only ink you should use in fountain pens. Waterproof ink is not necessarily permanent. It just resists water once dry. The ink is thicker than nonwaterproof and can clog the pen more easily, so it is important to keep your pen very clean while you work with this type of ink. Permanent ink resists the long-term effects of light on your lettering. Choosing a type of ink is a matter of trial and error—of finding something that feels right in your pen, doesn't clog it, and flows comfortably on the paper that you are using. Read the bottles

figure 3

For the Italic alphabet, a broad-edged pen is held at a 45-degree angle to the paper. The pen moves downward (from top to bottom) or sideways (from left to right) to create thick lines. Diagonal strokes, moving up and to the right, create hairlines.

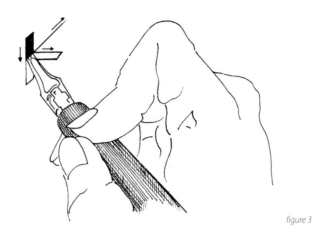

pen widths

ascender
waistline
x-height
baseline
descender

} 3
} 5
} 3

hearts adg ABC

ascender

descender

figure 3

and speak to a sales person for recommendations on the brands they have available.

Colored inks are more difficult to use than black. They are very thin and sometimes transparent, making it hard to get even coverage if you are working on a large area. Metallic ink must be thoroughly blended before each use as the suspended metallic particles settle to the bottom quickly. Any ink should be stirred well before beginning your project.

Many calligraphers use watercolor paint thinned with distilled water for more control and opacity in their lettering. Watercolors can be transparent, translucent, or opaque. Gouache is one of the most popular, and permanent, watercolor paints, valued for its opacity and luminosity of color.

LOADING THE PEN

The pen nib can be dipped into the inkwell to load the reservoir or can be loaded with a brush as described previously. Too much ink in

the reservoir will flow too quickly from the pen, leaving, at best, lines that are not crisp or, even worse, ink blobs. Not enough ink will cause the pen to skip and drag on the paper, creating a choppy line. It is a good idea to take a few practice strokes after each refill of the reservoir until you are sure that the ink flow is properly regulated.

CLEANING THE PEN

Clean your pen regularly by soaking it in warm, mildly sudsy water if using nonwaterproof ink, or use a commercial pen cleaner. If the reservoirs are removable, clean them separately. Waterproof inks dry quickly, so clean your pen often. Before dipping again in ink, make sure that your nib is completely dry and that no lint remains on the writing edge.

PAPER

The finest papers are made from linen or cotton rags, and the rag content indicates the quality and durability of the paper. Handmade papers generally have a uniform strength that resists tearing, while machine-made paper has a grain and is more easily torn in one direction.

The surface of paper is sized with a solution so that it doesn't soak up the ink like a blotter. Then a surface finish is applied. It will be difficult to work on paper that is too shiny, has too much texture, or has a surface that is too rough. Paper has a right and wrong side: the watermark can be read on the right side. Experiment with the paper/ink/pen combination until you find something you like.

PRINTING YOUR WORK

Your home computer may have a laser or ink-jet printer suitable for what you wish to accomplish, but sometimes it's preferable to have your work printed professionally. Engraving, the most formal method, creates a raised impression on the paper that can actually be felt on either side. Thermography is a much less-expensive method that imitates engraving by fusing a resin to the ink before it dries, creating a shiny, raised effect for the letters. Offset lithography produces lettering that is flat to the page with a matte finish. Letterpress is also a relief process. Unlike engraving, which raises the letters on the page, letterpress presses the letters into the paper.

Check with the printer for requirements for the finished artwork. Remember that if you wish to add color to the text, you still need to provide a mechanical (a page of text and/or art that is ready to be reproduced) in black type. Then select an ink color for the printer to apply.

ANATOMY OF AN ALPHABET

Dissecting and understanding the letters of each alphabet is critical to creating them. Each has distinguishing features and is made of basic parts. Look at the example shown on page 13. *(figure 3)* The x-height, also known as body height, is the main portion of a lowercase letter,

without including ascenders or descenders. It rests on the baseline and extends to the waistline (or headline). The descender is a portion of the letter that falls below the baseline, while the ascender is a portion of the letter that rises above the waistline. Letters are created with a series of strokes. Because of the nature of a calligraphy pen, the strokes must follow a certain direction. A map showing the direction and order of the strokes is called a ductus. A ductus is provided with each of the alphabets in this book.

With broad-edged pen alphabets, the size of the letters is based on the size of the pen. X-height, ascenders, and descenders are all defined by pen widths. *(figure 4)*

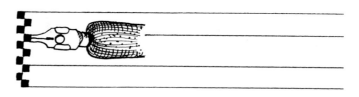

figure 4   ILLUSTRATIONS/CALLIGRAPHY BY SUSAN L. RAMSEY

Altering the size of the pen nib used to create a letter will alter its appearance just as much as if you altered the letter height. *(figure 5)*

Romance

Romance

Romance

figure 5

CALLIGRAPHY BY BEVERLY WLADOWSKI

figure 5

Each word is written at the same size, using a broad-edged pen with successively smaller nibs.

The other defining characteristics of broad-edged pen alphabets are the pen angle and the letter angle. For example, holding the pen at a 45-degree angle to the writing surface creates the thick lines in an Italic alphabet. The pen is then either pulled down or to the side. If the pen is moved along the same 45-degree angle as its orientation, only the thin, chiseled edge comes in contact with the paper, creating a hairline. In addition, the letters are slanted between 5 and 10 degrees to the right, and this also affects how much of the pen comes into contact with the paper. Look at each broad-edged alphabet to determine if the characters are slanted or upright, and experiment with your pen angle until the letters look right. *(figure 6)*

In general, fine-tipped pen alphabets are written at a slope of approximately 54 degrees. This varies somewhat from alphabet to alphabet. The severity of this angle is the reason that the oblique pen nib or penholder was developed—merely for comfort and control. These letters are made up of swells, shades, and connectives *(see figure 2)*. The pen nib can only flex a certain amount to make swells. The turns or loops of the letters must be round, not sharp or pointy *(figure 7)*.

PRACTICE MAKES PERFECT

Guide sheets or ruled paper can be purchased to help guide your hand, or you can create your own. In the beginning, it is easier to practice with larger letters. Make sure that the descenders from one line are not touching the ascenders from the line below it. Leave a margin of blank space around the top, bottom, and sides of the paper as well. Create guidelines using a ruler or T-square, measuring the parallel lines, and drawing them across the page in pencil. Mark the beginning of each x-height space to guide your hand to the next line.

Put a sheet of clean paper underneath your hand, so that you don't smudge the lettering or get grease on the page. Begin by making a series of straight, vertical lines. Write each stroke twenty to thirty times. Next, repeat the exercise with horizontal lines. Then move on to circles. Begin to write words and sentences, seeing how they flow on the page. It's always good to warm up your hand on scrap paper with these exercises, even after you have become proficient.

Lettering larger documents is difficult and must be done very slowly in order to avoid spelling mistakes or skipped letters and words. Mask your master copy with another piece of paper so that you are only looking at the line you are working on. Once your lettering is in place, assess the page. Is it well-balanced? Have you distinguished the most important words? Should you add flourishes, decorative rules, or graphics? Take this slow. It's easy to overdo. Lay a piece of tracing paper over your work and test out your idea before applying pen to paper.

Allow the ink to dry thoroughly before erasing any pencil marks. Give it at least an hour. Sometimes several hours are needed. Erase carefully with short, controlled movements in areas between letters and strokes. Now sit back and admire your work. You have created a unique piece of calligraphy for your wedding.

figure 6

The ideal pen angle varies from alphabet to alphabet. For the upright Will Rogers alphabet, shown here, a 40-degree angle works best.

ILLUSTRATIONS/CALLIGRAPHY
BY CHRISTOPHER WATKINS

figure 6

figure 7

An oblique pen holder is shown here.

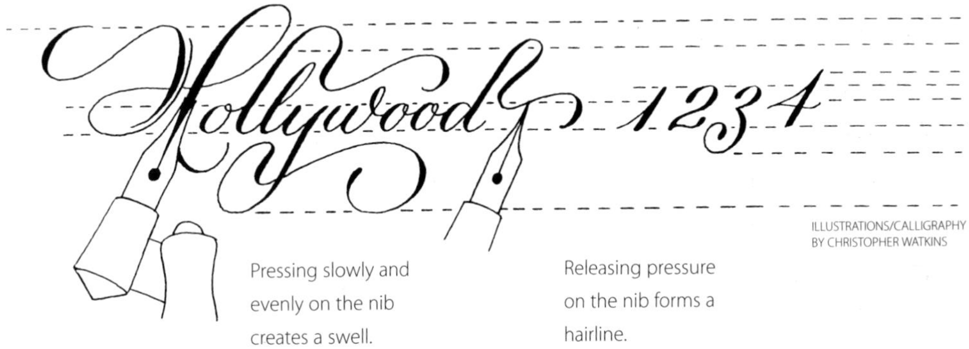

ILLUSTRATIONS/CALLIGRAPHY
BY CHRISTOPHER WATKINS

Pressing slowly and evenly on the nib creates a swell.

Releasing pressure on the nib forms a hairline.

figure 7

CLASSIC

Anna Marie Lacroix
and
Ramone Miguel Perez
invite you to celebrate their engagement
Friday, the tenth of August
at seven o'clock in the evening

The Beaumont
One Chanterelle Circle

Stephen

Taylo

FOR
YOU

I am my beloved's and
my beloved is mine.
SONG OF SOLOMON 6:3

Jennifer and Michael
February 24, 2001

classic CALLIGRAPHY

Long before the printing press was invented, learned scribes spent countless hours studying the art of hand lettering. Only after years of practice would they be entrusted with preserving the words of scholars in the form of exquisite handwritten manuscripts. Successive civilizations developed new styles of lettering, building on their predecessors' artistry to suit a new function or aesthetic style.

Adapted to our modern alphabet, classic-style letterforms conjure up a sense of history, formality, and even sanctity. The alphabets presented in this chapter are stately, evoking feelings of reverence—perfect for the formality of a wedding. All use a broad pen nib to create the traditional letter shapes. The beginner may find it easier to start out with a broad-tipped calligraphy marker or a fountain pen. As you gain experience and confidence, draw inspiration from history and add picture blocks, colored borders, and letters that are enlarged and embellished to turn your wedding invitation into a timeless illuminated manuscript.

The Italic alphabet is one of the most commonly used for wedding calligraphy. A descendant of earlier, more laborious lettering styles, it became popular because it was relatively quick, requiring fewer lifts of the pen. To write in Italic script, a broad-edged pen is held at an angle between 35 and 45 degrees. The letters naturally slant toward the right with the pen angle. CALLIGRAPHER HILARY WILLIAMS

A B C D E F G H I
J K L M N O P Q
R S T U V W X Y Z
a b c d e f g h i j k l m
n o p q r s t u v w x y z
1 2 3 4 5 6 7 8 9 0

A B C D E F G H I

J K L M N O P Q

R S T U V W X Y Z

a b c d e f g h i j k l m

n o p q r s t u v w x y z

1 2 3 4 5 6 7 8 9 0

Uncial scripts, which date back to early Greek and Roman times, perfectly express the theme of a classic, modern-day wedding. The name "Uncial" (sounds like uhn-shul) means "inch" and was probably coined in reference to the large size of the lettering used in the decorative luxury books of the time. Many of our lowercase letters originate from this alphabet, and it is a good practice hand for beginners. CALLIGRAPHER
MELISSA DINWIDDIE

A B C D E F G H I J
K L M N O P Q R S
T U V W X Y & Z
1 2 3 4 5 6
7 8 9 & 0

ABCDEFGHIJ

KLMNOPQRS

TUVWXYZ

1 2 3 4 5 6

7 8 9 0

Blackletter, Textura Quadrata, and Old English are common names for this lettering style. A descendant of an early Gothic alphabet, the letters are notably angular and upright, appropriate for announcing a more formal event. Ancient scribes seemed more concerned with the script's overall graphic effect than with its readability. This version of the letterform recognizes the importance of maintaining legibility without losing the formality of the alphabet. CALLIGRAPHER MELISSA DINWIDDIE

ABCDEFGH
IJKLMNOPQ
RSTUVWXYZ
abcdefghijklm
nopqrstuvwxyz
1234567890

ABCDEFGH
IJKLMNOPQ
RSTUVWXYZ
abcdefghijklm
nopqrstuvwxyz
1234567890

vellum PLACE CARDS

Place cards let your guests know where to sit at the reception and present a perfect opportunity for using calligraphy at your wedding. This simple project is ideal for the beginner calligrapher. Variations on this project are also limitless for more experienced calligraphers. Cut the work in half by purchasing precut and prescored place cards at your local stationer or craft store. Vellum is a beautiful and forgiving paper choice for placing over your inscribed card. The translucent paper can jazz up a plain card or soften a lively design while masking slight imperfections. Vellum comes in various shades, colors, and patterns. Try a patterned card underneath a solid colored vellum, or experiment with colored inks and flourishes to match the vellum pattern.

MATERIALS

- purchased place cards made from lightweight card stock
- calligraphy fountain pen
- black ink cartridge
- patterned vellum
- glue stick or white craft glue
- soft eraser
- for variation: silver calligraphy marker, silver extra-fine-point marker, silver gel pen, plain vellum

ETIQUETTE ADVICE

At a formal event, cards directing guests to an assigned table or to individual seating assignments should have first and last names, as well as titles. In a more casual environment—a rehearsal dinner, an intimate or informal wedding, or the bride and groom's head table—first names only are acceptable.

1

TIPS AND TECHNIQUES

• Sometimes a slight ink smudge can be removed by gently scraping the top layer of the paper with a craft knife. Don't write on the surface after removing the smudge. The ink will bleed.

• Attach vellum to the back of a light-colored card with a glue stick or white craft glue. They both dry clear. When working with a dark-colored card, apply the glue smoothly to the entire back of the card for an even finish.

STEP 1 Cut cards to size, or use packaged place cards from a stationer. Determine the position of the baseline, measure carefully, and draw a pencil line lightly onto the face of the card. If needed, draw guidelines to indicate the x-height, ascenders, and descenders. Using a broad-nibbed fountain pen, calligraph the guest's name onto the card.

STEP 2 Allow the ink to dry thoroughly. Gently remove any smudges. Carefully erase the pencilled guidelines.

STEP 3 Cut the vellum into pieces the exact size of the place cards. For the best fit, fold the cards and the vellum separately. Use a bone folder or the back of a spoon to get a good, crisp crease.

2

3

VARIATION True beginners can obtain dramatic results with metallic calligraphy markers and gel pens. The broad shape of the nib and heavier nature of a felt-tipped marker can't reproduce the delicate lines of pen and ink, but a light hand and a flair for embellishment produce a pleasing artistic effect, with or without a vellum overlay.

wedding
READING KEEPSAKE

Keep the memories of your wedding alive by transforming a passage from your ceremony into a work of art you can look at every day. You can choose a portion of your vows, a reading, or a meaningful wedding poem or song. A toast or blessing offered at the event would also work nicely. A touch of gold ink in the lettering adds distinction. Use a precut mat to frame the inscription. Painting flowers in a trail from the lettered sheet onto the mat ties the two together.

MATERIALS

• watercolor paper

• acid-free precut mat board

• pencil

• ruler

• broad-edged calligraphy pen

• fine-tipped calligraphy pen

• paintbrush

• black ink

• gold ink

• watercolor paint

• soft eraser

• masking tape

• light box (optional, see Tips and Techniques)

• for variation: braided satin upholstery rope, hot glue gun,

  fabric glue, purchased photo or memory album

1

2

3

- If you do not have a light box, ink the letters directly over the initial pencil draft. Carefully erase the pencil lines once the ink has dried thoroughly.

- Press flowers from your wedding and attach them with diluted white glue or decoupage medium, instead of watercolor paint, to create the floral "bouquet."

- Any beautiful trim can be substituted to frame the text.

STEP 1 Cut the watercolor paper to fit the size of the mat opening, adding at least 1/2" (1 cm) on each edge for overlap. On a blank sheet of white paper, rule the working area that will show and add pencil rules to guide the size of the letters. Draft the words and flowers in pencil to work out the spacing.

STEP 2 Place the watercolor paper over the pencil draft on the light box. If needed, re-rule the pencil lines to guide the size of the letters. Using a fine-tipped pen, outline the first letter in black ink to create what is called an initial cap. Render the rest of the words in black ink, using a broad-edged pen.

STEP 3 Fill in the initial cap with gold ink. Add a dot of gold to the couple's names as a decorative element. Using a fine-tipped pen, add flourishes to the initial cap and first letters of the bride and groom's names, outlining the gold with a distinct shape. Paint the flowers on the watercolor paper.

VARIATION The same artwork creates a meaningful cover for a wedding photo album, memory book, or scrapbook. Attach the text sheet to the album using fabric glue or hot glue. Add a decorative border of upholstery trim using hot glue to give it a finished look.

f a v o r TAGS

Sending guests home with a token gift of appreciation has become a common practice at weddings. One way to personalize this gesture of gratitude is with calligraphic tags. Here, the gift tags are written in Uncial and are attached to small, geometric-shaped boxes. It is a good idea to place the favors on a table near the door for guests to take on their way out.

MATERIALS

• vellum

• white paper

• gift boxes

• 3/4" (2 cm) satin-edged ribbon—18" (46 cm) per favor

• pencil

• ruler

• broad-edged calligraphy pen

• black ink

• glue stick

• hot glue gun

• computer with scanner

• for variation: green, patterned vellum; gold paint marker; gold satin rope; hole punch

CALLIGRAPHER MELISSA DINWIDDIE
CRAFT ARTIST BETTE MATTHEWS

TIPS AND TECHNIQUES

- Although Uncial is a heavy lettering style, when crafted with a thinner nib it looks delicate enough to pair with ornamental embellishments.

- A dab of hot glue on the ribbon's knot will keep it from opening accidentally.

- Try different pen nibs to test various weights for the final text.

STEP 1 Using the white paper, a pencil, and a ruler, draw the shape of the gift box and render the text.

STEP 2 Using a computer scanner, scan the renderings and delete the bottom tip of the cone. (A photocopier also works if you do not have access to a computer.) If you are trying more than one rendering or lettering weight, cut out both and place each on a favor box to see which looks better. Duplicate the tag of choice on the vellum, print the necessary quantity, and cut out the tags.

STEP 3 Fill a favor box and close it. Tie the ribbon into a bow at the top of the box. Use hot glue to adhere the wavy tails of the ribbon to the box. Attach the tag to the box using a glue stick. Be careful not to smudge the type.

VARIATION For variation, print the tags on colored, patterned vellum and cut out in a circle shape. Add a beautiful edge to the tag with a gold paint marker. Use a hole punch to create an opening. Pair with a different shaped box and gold satin rope instead of ribbon to completely change the appearance of this favor.

engagement
PARTY INVITATION

As soon as the engagement is announced, the parties for the couple begin. Choose an invitation style that is appropriate for the event, or even one that reflects the party location. Imitate the design of an illuminated manuscript and create a beautiful picture block paired with a classic, Blackletter text style. For this invitation, stationery was purchased with the graphic design preprinted on the paper and envelopes. After printing the invitation text, the sheet is trimmed to its final size.

MATERIALS

• grid paper

• white paper

• paper with preprinted graphic design

• matching envelope

• broad-edged calligraphy pen

• black ink

• spray mount

• computer with scanner

• for variation: clip art, white card, cream card

Anna⁊
and
Ramon

1

- Decorative papers can be purchased by the sheet at fine paper or stationery stores.

- Add a touch of gold to the design or to the lettering with gold calligraphy ink, a gold gel pen, or a gold paint pen.

- Rather than using a copy to paste up a centered mechanical, the rendered text can also be scanned into the computer and centered in a layout program.

Anni Marie La
and
Ramone Miguel

2

Anna Marie Lacroix
and
Ramone Miguel Perez
invite you to celebrate their engagement
friday, the tenth of August
at seven o'clock in the evening

The Beaumont
One Chanterelle Circle

3

STEP 1 Working on grid paper at a comfortable working size, render each line of text for the final invitation. Align all rows at the left.

STEP 2 Make a good copy of the text on clean, white paper. Cut out each line. Using spray mount, center each line on a new sheet of grid paper to create a mechanical.

STEP 3 Scan the mechanical into the computer and reduce the text to the final size. Align the text so that it will fit on the paper in alignment with the preprinted artwork. Print the invitation.

VARIATION Instead of using paper with a preprinted design, create a picture block on plain paper with clip art. The look of the invitation will change dramatically based on the type of art selected and the color of paper and text.

wedding invitation
ETIQUETTE

In years past, the wedding invitation was a formal document that followed a strict formula in terms of its appearance and wording. Today, many couples still choose the classic invitation for their event. A variety of choices, however, are available—and appropriate—for a twenty-first century wedding. For most guests, the invitation is the first—and sometimes only—indication they'll receive about the style and formality of a wedding. Yours should reflect your personality as well as the wedding style, both in the presentation and the phrasing of the invitation.

Society's prescription for nuptial celebrations was clear-cut in previous decades. The bride's parents were the hosts, and the invitation came from them. A guest receiving a formal invitation for an event beginning after 6:00 P.M. understood that black tie was the appropriate attire, so it was unnecessary to include such a notation in the text. The invitation might request an R.s.v.p., and the guest would respond on his or her personal stationery. The invitation itself was for the wedding ceremony; if the guest was also invited to a reception, a separate reception card was included in the mailing.

Many of these customs are still utilized in the most formal of settings, but new standards of invitation etiquette have evolved to include a broader range of possibilities, reflective of the casual atmosphere of life today. Our modern social climate dictates that etiquette should be used as a guide only, rather than as a set of unbreakable rules. If your style is informal, or your wedding is informal, your invitation need not conform to any rules as long as all the necessary information is present and easy for the guest to understand.

SAMPLES OF INVITATION WORDING

THE BRIDE'S PARENTS HOST:
Mr. and Mrs. Matthew Beatty
request the honour of your presence
at the marriage of their daughter
Eliza Brook
to
Mr. Antoine Michel Richieu
Saturday, the fifth of June
at half after five o'clock
The Lynbrook Society for Ethical Culture
Lynbrook, New York

Reception following the ceremony

THE GROOM'S PARENTS HOST:
Mr. and Mrs. Jerard Richieu
request the honour of your presence
at the marriage of
Miss Eliza Brook Beatty
to their son
Antoine Michel Richieu
etc.

**THE BRIDE'S PARENTS HOST AND
THE GROOM'S PARENTS ARE INCLUDED:**
Mr. and Mrs. Matthew Beatty
request the honour of your presence
at the marriage of their daughter
Eliza Brook
to
Mr. Antoine Michel Richieu
son of Mr. and Mrs. Jerard Richieu
etc.

DIVORCED PARENTS HOST:
Mrs. Leanora Beatty
and
Mr. Matthew Beatty
request the honour of your presence
at the marriage of their daughter
Eliza Brook
to
Mr. Antoine Michel Richieu
etc.

DIVORCED AND REMARRIED PARENTS HOST:

Dr. and Mrs. John Hurst Lake
and
Mr. Matthew Beatty
request the honour of your presence
at the marriage of their daughter
Eliza Brook
to
Mr. Antoine Michel Richieu
etc.

BOTH SETS OF PARENTS HOST:

Mr. and Mrs. Matthew Beatty
and
Mr. and Mrs. Jerard Richieu
request the honour of your presence
at the marriage of their children
Eliza Brook
and
Antoine Michel
etc.

THE BRIDE AND GROOM HOST:

The honour of your presence is requested
at the marriage of
Eliza Brook Beatty
and
Antoine Michel Richieu
etc.

THE COUPLE HOSTS AND THE PARENTS ARE INCLUDED:

Together with their parents
Eliza Brook Beatty
and
Antoine Michel Richieu
request the honour of your presence
at their marriage
etc.

NONTRADITIONAL WORDING:

Eliza Brook Beatty
and
Antoine Michel Richieu
invite you to celebrate our wedding
or
invite you to gather in community
to witness and celebrate their marriage
or
invite you to share the joy
as we exchange marriage vows
or
invite you to dance at our wedding
etc.
or
Please join
Eliza Brook Beatty
and
Antoine Michel Richieu
at the celebration of their marriage
etc.

INVITATION ETIQUETTE TIPS

• As a standard rule of thumb, the people who pay for the wedding are mentioned on the invitation. Many couples, however, choose to honor parents by including their names, even if the parents are not making a financial contribution to the event.

• Write names out in full on an invitation or an envelope. Titles, such as Mister or Doctor, may be abbreviated.

• Traditionally, if the ceremony location is a house of worship, the phrase "request the honour of your presence" is used. When the ceremony takes place in a secular location, the phrase of choice is "request the pleasure of your company."

• The Anglican spelling of "honour" and "favour" is commonly used on wedding invitations, but "honor" or "favor" is perfectly acceptable.

• Spell out dates and times. Avoid using the abbreviations "P.M." or "A.M." For a starting time after 6:00 P.M., use the phrase "in the evening."

• Including the year after the date and the city after the location is optional.

• If your ceremony and reception are in the same location, a separate reception card is unnecessary. In the text, beneath the ceremony details, note "Reception immediately following."

• It is permissible to write R.s.v.p. in all capital letters, but this looks awkward in most scripts or calligraphic alphabets. Place this notation in the lower left corner of the invitation. If you are including a response card, do not include an R.s.v.p. notation in the invitation text.

• If a particular dress code is requested for the event, place the information in the lower right corner of the invitation. "Black tie," "Black tie encouraged," "Black tie optional," or "Casual attire welcomed" are all acceptable phrases.

• Send your invitations four to six weeks prior to the wedding. If you have international guests or many guests travelling a long distance, add two weeks. Guests are asked to respond one to two weeks prior to the event.

• Number your guest list. When sending out invitations, write in the guest's corresponding number on the back of each response card in pencil. That way, if someone forgets to write his name on the front of the response card, you can identify the guest by the number on your master list.

• To assemble, the enclosures are stacked face up on top of the invitation in the following order: the reception card, the response card (which should be slid under its envelope flap, not inserted into the envelope), and then any additional inserts, such as a pew card or driving directions. Insert the invitation and enclosures into the inner envelope (if using one), and insert the entire package into the outer envelope.

Elegant

Mr. and Mrs. Nicholas Carroll
145 Dearborn Street
Chicago, Illinois 60623

Mr. and Mrs. Nicholas Carroll
145 Dearborn Street
Chicago, Illinois 60623

Mr. and Mrs. Nicholas Carroll
145 Dearborn Street
Chicago, Illinois 60623

Table Five

Please join
at a rehearsal din
in honor of

Lauren and Jim

Friday, the first of May
at five o'clock
Sundial Resort

Table

elegant CALLIGRAPHY

CALLIGRAPHER SUSAN L. RAMSEY

As a result of efforts to work more efficiently and to produce documents intended for daily use, alphabets branched out in many stylistic directions. Yet the general trend was towards a more flowing motion, culminating in the sinuous scripts of seventeenth-, eighteenth-, and nineteenth-century Europe. The advent of paper also allowed changes in options for both pen and ink, and new technologies spurred the development of the printed word.

Three alphabets are included in this chapter. When striving for elegance in your wedding, remember that an understated style sometimes has the biggest impact. Each of these refined alphabets is perfectly suited to an elegant style. French Gothic, created with the broad-edged pen, retains a sense of formality. Its thick and thin lines are formed by the angle of the pen and by the direction of the pen stroke. The other two—Bickham and Rook—are cousins, both created using the pointed pen. They originate from the copperplate-engraved texts used to teach basic writing skills. With a pointed pen, applied pressure, or lack thereof, is used to create the thick swells and delicate, thin lines common to this type of calligraphy.

In its heyday, the pointed pen was used for daily correspondence. It was commonly used with alphabets that reflected fine penmanship as much as fine calligraphy. Practice writing the letters with a pencil first, to get used to the shape of the letters and to be able to write them smoothly. The projects in this chapter show a variety of uses for the elegant lettering styles. They also would work as well with any of the other alphabets in this book.

All scripts created with a fine-tipped calligraphy pen are similar in the way the letters are formed. Differences are subtle and may be noted in the flourishes of the capital letters, the ascenders, and the descenders. The thickness of lines is determined by the pressure applied to the strokes, not by the angle of the pen. This hand, based on a typeface known as Rook, uses round letters with loops in the capitals and long ascenders and descenders in the lowercase letters. It is a classic choice for an elegant wedding. CALLIGRAPHER NAN DELUCA

A B C D E F G H

I J K L M N O P Q

R S T U V W X Y Z

a b c d e f g h i j k l m

n o p q r s t u v w x y z

1 2 3 4 5 6 7 8 9 0

A B C D E F G H
I J K L M N O P Q
R S T U V W X Y Z
a b c d e f g h i j k l m
n o p q r s t u v w x y z
1 2 3 4 5 6 7 8 9 0

In the eighteenth century, master penman and engraver George Bickham published a book showing samples of his work and that of other masters from his time and previous centuries. It is still used today as a leading reference for script lettering and is an ideal choice for an elegant wedding. This alphabet honors him by bearing his name, Bickham. As with other script alphabets, it is created with a pointed pen, relying on pressure to produce the characteristic thick and thin lines. Its tailored capital letters rely on graceful swashes rather than looped flourishes; some of the lowercase letters have straight, rather than looped, descenders. CALLIGRAPHER
SUSAN L. RAMSEY

A B C D E F G H
I J K L M N O P Q
R S T U V W X Y Z

a b c d e f g h i j k l m

n o p q r s t u v w x y z

1 2 3 4 5 6 7 8 9 0

A B C D E F G H
I J K L M N O P Q
R S T U V W X Y Z
a b c d e f g h i j k l m
n o p q r s t u v w x y z
1 2 3 4 5 6 7 8 9 0

In the French Gothic, or Bâtarde, alphabet, the capitals are wide and round, with a fluidity of motion. Paired with closely packed lowercase letters, the effect is well-balanced. For this alphabet, use a broad-edged pen held at a 45-degree angle to the paper. A combination of this angle and the upright nature of the letters creates a heavy character that is sure to make your invitation and other wedding correspondence stand out.

CALLIGRAPHER SUSAN L. RAMSEY

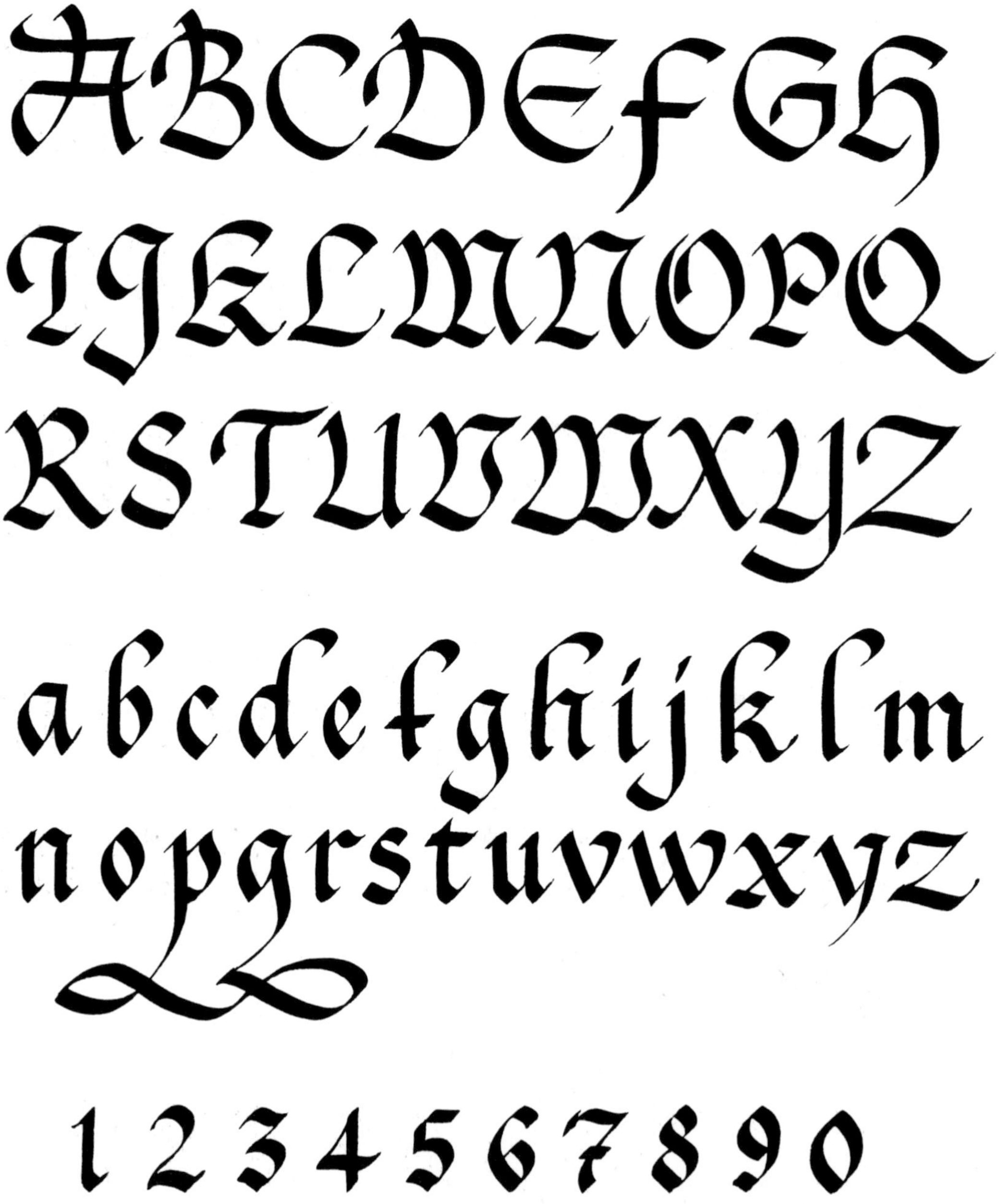

ABCDEFGH
IJKLMNOPQ
RSTUVWXYZ

abcdefghijklm
nopqrstuvwxyz

1234567890

ABCDEFGH
IJKLMNOPQ
RSTUVWXYZ

abcdefghijklm
nopqrstuvwxyz

1234567890

r e h e a r s a l   d i n n e r
I N V I T A T I O N

There's no need to sacrifice elegance for a less formal event. A more relaxed event should still be announced with style. Here, a red, deckled edge emboldens a butter-colored card. For a small party, each card can be written by hand with beautiful script. Otherwise, scan an original hand-rendered invitation to duplicate. If you cannot find stationery with a border like the one shown here, you can apply a border to plain card stock and coordinating envelopes with calligraphy ink, paint, or even a metallic paint pen.

MATERIALS

for invitation with red, deckled edge:

- purchased card stock
- matching envelope
- fine-tipped pen
- black ink

for invitation with peach ribbon:

- petal paper
- vellum
- 1/8" (3 mm) wide peach satin ribbon —2 feet (61 cm) per invitation
- fine-tipped pen
- black ink
- hole punch
- computer with scanner

for invitation with white bow:

- patterned paper
- coordinating solid-colored paper
- vellum
- 3/8" (9 mm) wide white organza ribbon—1 foot (30 cm) per invitation
- fine-tipped pen
- black ink
- glue stick
- hole punch
- computer with scanner

for invitation with pressed flowers:

- watercolor paper
- pressed flower petals
- patterned art tissue paper
- white craft glue
- small, soft paintbrush
- fine-tipped pen
- black ink
- computer with scanner

for booklet variation:

- petal paper
- white paper
- 1/8" (3 mm) wide light green satin ribbon—18" (46 cm) per invitation
- fine-tipped pen
- black ink
- glue stick
- computer with scanner

Please join us at a rehearsal dinner in honor of Lauren and Jim Friday, the first of May at five o'clock Sundial Resort Sanibel, Florida Bill and Sue Evans R.s.v.p. 555-1234

VERSION 1 For this version, render the text, scan it into the computer, and print onto the vellum. Cut both the vellum and a sheet of petal paper to 4" x 8" (10 cm x 20 cm) in size. Place the printed vellum on top of the petal paper, and punch a series of small holes through both sheets at the top. Weave ribbon through the holes finishing with a bow on the left-hand side.

VERSION 2 Vellum softens the effect of the type here. Print the text onto patterned paper and mount it on a coordinating solid-colored paper using a glue stick. Allow for a 1/8" (3 mm) border. Cut a piece of vellum 1/4" (6 mm) shorter in length and width than the patterned paper and place it over the patterned paper. Punch two small holes at the top of the invitation, puncturing through all three sheets. Weave a white organza ribbon through the holes and finish with a petite bow.

VERSION 3 For this invitation, the text is printed onto watercolor paper that has been cut to size. Pressed flowers are adhered to the invitation with a diluted solution of white craft glue and water. Lightly brush glue solution on the backside of the flower. The invitation is wrapped in a patterned art tissue paper, allowing for a 1/2" (1 cm) overlap in front. Another pressed flower is glued to the front to keep the tissue closed.

VARIATION Create a booklet with the folded invitation inside. Use a glue stick to attach the invitation inside of the petal paper cover. Add a decorative ribbon along the spine.

elegant ENVELOPES

Calligraphy is frequently used to address an invitation envelope, whether the invitation itself has been penned by hand or produced by a printer. Although all styles of calligraphy look beautiful, penned script is probably requested most often for envelopes. Addresses may be placed centered, staggered, or flush left on the envelope.

MATERIALS

• envelopes

• guide sheet

• fine-tipped calligraphy pen

• black ink

• light box

• for variation: burgundy ink

ETIQUETTE ADVICE

Although some people choose to use a computer to address envelopes, simple, beautiful penmanship is preferable and far more personal. Other than titles, such as Mr., Mrs., and Dr., all names and words should be spelled out and not abbreviated. Although it is acceptable to abbreviate junior or senior (capitalizing the first letter of each), the most formal envelope would present the words spelled out in lowercase.

TIPS AND TECHNIQUES

• A heavy rule will show through a standard envelope, but a lined envelope will require working on a light box in order to see the inserted guide sheet. Alternatively, envelope lining can sometimes be removed—very carefully—and reinserted after the envelope has been addressed. This is extremely tedious and risks tearing the envelope or lining.

Mr. and Mrs. Nicholas Carroll
145 Dearborn Street
Chicago, Illinois
6 0 6 2 3

2

Mr and Mrs Nicholas Carroll
145 Dearborn Street
Chicago, Illinois 60623

3

STEP 1 Draft a test envelope to work out the size and spacing of the letters and the lines. Once a pleasing arrangement has been determined, create a guide sheet of heavy lines, either with a marker or on a computer. Insert the guide sheet into the envelope. Determine the guideline that falls closest to the center of the envelope. This marks where the first line of the address should be placed. If an address contains a long line and you are using a staggered layout, the angle of the diagonal layout can be adjusted.

STEP 2 The zip code can be placed on the same line as the city and state, but sometimes it appears better when placed separately. Spreading out the spacing of the zip code looks very elegant.

STEP 3 Writing too close to any of the edges of the envelope is a common mistake. For an address with long lines, begin the first line more to the left, use a smaller angle for the diagonal layout, or drop the zip code down to a fourth line. Another common error is to place the address too high on the envelope. It will look better if the first line is centered both horizontally and vertically.

VARIATION You can use colored ink and understated flourishes to enrich the envelope without sacrificing the degree of formality.

reception
TABLE NUMBERS

The days of institutional numbers skewered onto stark, spiky metal holders to designate tables are over. The number on the table should be as beautiful as the place card itself, and calligraphy is a handsome way to achieve this effect.

The numbers can be displayed in many ways. Using folded cardstock, you can prop them as is. Small holders can be used for a more upright presentation. Or insert the inscribed paper into an elegant frame appropriate to the décor. Embellished with flourishes, the couple's new monogram, or a painted leaf or flower, these numbers do not have to be whisked away and hidden after the guests are seated.

MATERIALS

- paper or cardstock
- decorative frame
- table number holder or place card holder
- fine-tipped calligraphy pen
- fine brush
- black ink
- gold ink
- colored ink
- watercolor paint
- light box

ETIQUETTE ADVICE

Creating table assignments for guests is a thoughtful amenity. Although time-consuming (as well as thought provoking) for the wedding planner, it eliminates the need for guests to jockey for position upon arriving at the reception. It also rules out the possibility that Aunt Zelda may end up sitting by herself with your college sorority sisters because there was no room left at the family table.

VERSION 1 A number can stand alone nicely, but a bit of abstract watercolor flora makes a nice embellishment.

TIPS AND TECHNIQUES

- Because the table numbers must be readily visible, a fine-tipped calligraphy pen cannot create swells large enough to be proportionate to the necessary size of the numeral or lettering. There is a very simple solution to this. Render the text at normal size, enlarge it with a copier, and use a light box to trace the enlarged text onto the final card. Outline the letters or numbers and fill them in with ink with either a pen or a fine brush.

- Arrange tables in numerical order in the reception room so guests can find their spot with ease.

VERSION 2 Another option is to spell out the numeral and use color and art to tie into a theme. In this example, the card was designed for a seaside wedding.

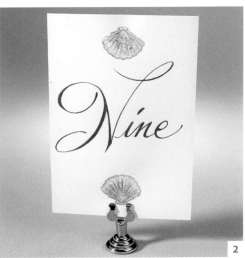

VERSION 3 Add the word "Table" to fill out the card. Flourishes and scrolls enhance the visual appeal.

VARIATION Glue the menu into a folded card and have the table number do double duty.

CALLIGRAPHER SUSAN L. RAMSEY

wedding
ANNOUNCEMENT

It's not uncommon to send an announcement after the wedding to acquaintances that were not invited to the event. The wedding announcement follows the basic format and wording of a wedding invitation and can vary in style in the same way. In the most formal style, the bride's parents announce their daughter's marriage to the groom, including the date and place of the wedding. This announcement was embellished with a graceful rubber stamp after it was printed on ecru card stock. A matching envelope is addressed using the same lettering style.

MATERIALS

• white paper

• ecru card stock

• pencil

• ruler

• broad-edged calligraphy pen

• black ink

• light box

• computer with scanner

• rubber stamp

• black stamp pad

• for variation: clear stamp pad, gold embossing powder

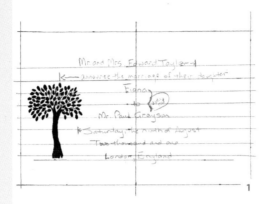

1

- Mistakes are easy to correct on projects that use the computer. Scan in corrections with patches of new text.

- The ink must be wet for embossing powder to stick to it, so work quickly. Do not overheat the powder: as soon as the gold begins to look glossy, remove it from the heat source.

Mr. and Mrs. Edw announce the marriage of Fiona

2

Mr. and Mrs. Edward Taylor
announce the marriage of their daughter
Fiona
to
Mr. Paul Grayson
Saturday, the ninth of August
Two thousand and one
London, England

3

STEP 1 Create a draft in pencil to work out the horizontal and vertical layout of the page. If adding any form of artwork to the final piece, include it in the draft to allow enough space for it.

STEP 2 Working on a light box, place a sheet of white paper over the pencil draft. Render the text.

STEP 3 When the text is finished, scan it into the computer. Print out the announcements on good card stock and trim to fit in the envelopes.

VARIATION Instead of stamping the design in black ink, use clear ink and immediately cover it with gold embossing powder. Tap off the excess and heat the embossed design until the powder is activated and begins to puff.

working with a
PROFESSIONAL
CALLIGRAPHER

Despite the best of intentions, sometimes the bride has little time to pursue a new course of learning, such as calligraphy, or to personally hand-letter envelopes, create last-minute place cards, etc. Instead, a bride may delegate the lettering of her wedding stationery to an experienced calligrapher. Choosing a professional to create all or part of the wedding stationery is a wise course of action in many instances. A professional understands the importance of the event and can handle it with expertise.

FINDING A CALLIGRAPHER

As with many wedding services, word of mouth is a great way to locate a trustworthy professional. Ask anyone you know who recently hosted or attended an event. Your reception hall, a local stationer, or wedding salon may also be of help. Look for ads or listings in regional wedding magazines. The Internet also offers a vast amount of information. For noteworthy web sites and other sources, including some of the book's contributors, refer to the Calligraphy Resources section on page 124. Don't feel as if you are confined to local sources only. With the ease of overnight delivery, fax, phone, and e-mail, any calligrapher is within your reach.

GUIDELINES

Have a clear idea of what you want before approaching the calligrapher. Artists often have portfolios of their work and can present you with new ideas, but it is important to know what you like first.

Be organized! The clearer your instructions, the more likely that the job will proceed without a hitch. Have every word on your address list correspond exactly with the way it is to be rendered. For example, write out "Mr. and Mrs." rather than using an ampersand. Write out "Street" and "Avenue" rather than abbreviating them, and spell out the names of states. Proofread your list before giving it to the calligrapher. Likewise, proofread their work before giving your final okay to the job.

COSTS AND CONTRACTS

Pricing varies greatly from region to region and artist to artist. Also, the cost of your work is dependent on what that work is. For example, hiring the calligrapher to create a master mechanical for your wedding invitation will have one cost. Contracting with the person to oversee the printing process will naturally be more expensive. Having the artist render each invitation individually will be even more costly. Choosing a design from the calligrapher's portfolio may be more cost-effective than asking for a completely new design. Hiring someone at the last minute will likely involve rush fees. Contracting with someone and canceling at a later date will sometimes result in a kill fee, or a loss of your deposit. Get a firm price quote in writing from the calligrapher and outline the entire job in a contract. This provides protection for both parties, clarifies the expectations, and helps avoid disappointment. Make sure the payment structure is clear and agreeable before signing a final contract. Some people require a deposit. Others may ask for a full payment prior to or upon delivering the finished work.

• Maintain realistic expectations. Many calligraphers are willing to match a typeface or imitate someone else's style, but calligraphy is similar to handwriting. Every person's penmanship is a little bit different.

• Look at the calligrapher's work and ask for samples, as quality and skill vary greatly.

• Book ahead! Calligraphers' schedules get busy, especially at certain times of year. Line up a calligrapher at least a month in advance of when you need the work done. Sooner is even better. Some calligraphers are booked several months in advance.

Romantic

...mance...

...ic love happens; it is not ...ght about; one falls in love.

Robin and Erik
September 8, 2001

Heart

What comes from the heart goes to the heart.

...bin and E...
...ember 8...

Promise

Love is a promise to ...
souvenir, once given ...

Happiness

Happiness comes from ...
loving than being loved.

Robin and Erik
September 8, 2001

...have
...our friends
...u are invited to

and

...u we exchange...

Menu

Mixed Green Salad with Vegetables
&
Cold Poached Salmon with Dill Sauce
Orange Roughy with Beurre Blanc Sauce

romantic CALLIGRAPHY

CALLIGRAPHER HILARY WILLIAMS

The development of the printing press had profound impact on the penned word. Engravers, attempting to copy the work of calligraphers, developed a script style that, in turn, the calligraphers learned to copy with a fine-tipped pen. These scripts were sometimes embellished to the point of being illegible, and reflected the elaborate lifestyles favored by the upper classes in the seventeenth, eighteenth, and nineteenth centuries. The romance and grace of the earlier alphabets, however, was not lost. Artist William Morris brought the Italic hand back into the public eye in the late 1800s.

Calligraphy is romantic in and of itself, but the addition of embellishment, either in the letters or in the materials used, dresses up the printed word. The foundation for all pointed-pen script alphabets, Copperplate, is shown in this chapter, along with one of its offshoots. The letters for both scripts can be embellished with practice. The broad-edged, flourished Italic in this chapter is a romantic version of its simpler parent, adding a free-flowing swash to the Italic groundwork. Four projects in this chapter show beautiful applications for these romantic hands, from the simple menu, designed to make your guests' experience more pleasurable, to a collection of ideas for decorating place cards.

Italic refers to a slanted calligraphy form originally developed in the fourteenth and fifteenth centuries, that usually has connectives between the letters. The name Chancery Cursive is often used interchangeably, although it is a more ornate version of an Italic script. This flourished Italic is the calligrapher's own version of a Chancery Cursive and is sure to make an impression on your guests. The character of the flourishes and connectives adds deep drama to the letters without altering the basic structure or readability of the letters.

CALLIGRAPHER   BEVERLY WLADKOWSKI

A B C D E F G H
I J K L M N O P Q
R S T U V W X Y Z
a b c d e f g h i j k l m
n o p q r s t u v w x y z
1 2 3 4 5 6 7 8 9 0

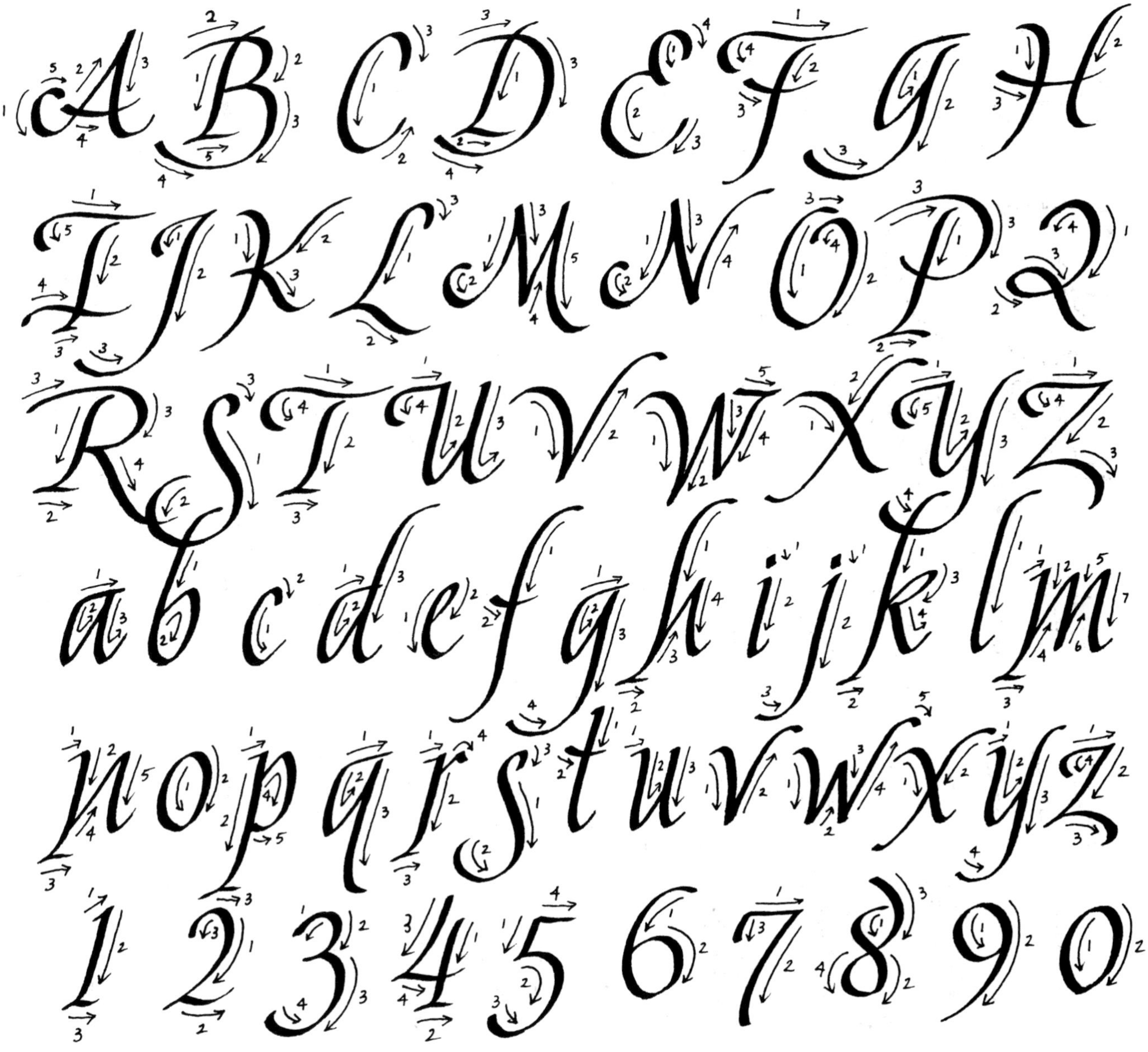

Copperplate script developed in conjunction with the invention of the printing press. Trying to duplicate the calligraphy of the penned word, engravers discovered quickly that they were better off designing a typeface specifically for their technology. The printing plates, engraved on sheets of copper with a pointed tool, created a new, even lettering form with delicate strokes, swells, and flourishes. Calligraphers gave up their broad-edged pen nibs and developed the pointed pen, with its fine-tipped nib, to copy the style of the copper plate engravings. In its simplest form or its most embellished—with ornate loops and swirls—Copperplate is a lovely choice for a romantic affair. CALLIGRAPHER HILARY WILLIAMS

A B C D E F G H I
J K L M N O P Q
R S T U V W X Y Z

a b c d e f g h i j k l m
n o p q r s t u v w x y z

1 2 3 4 5 6 7 8 9 0

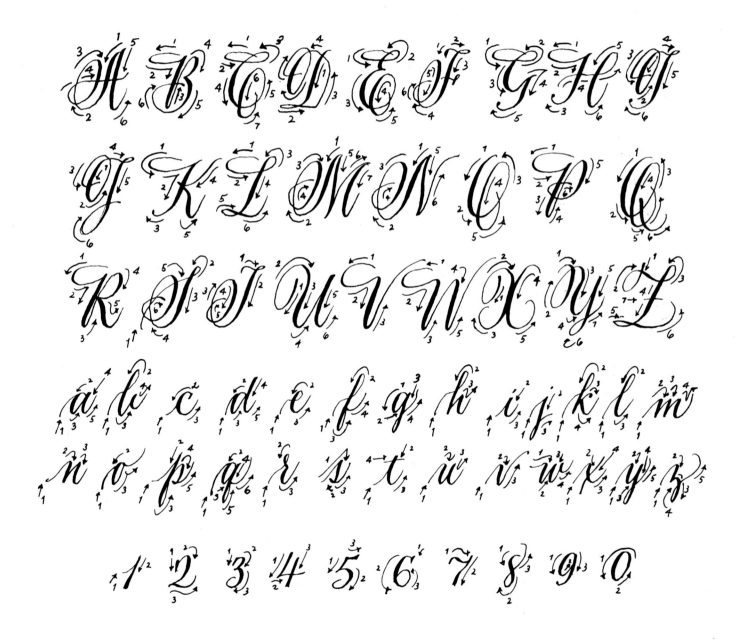

Another form of Copperplate, Spencerian is a rich, flowing script, perfectly symbolic of romance. For this particular alphabet, the pen rarely leaves the page and requires much practice to master the letters' graceful, fluid motion. As with other Copperplate scripts, the differences are seen mainly in the flourished capital letters as well as in the ascenders and descenders. CALLIGRAPHER HILARY WILLIAMS

A B C D E F G H I

J K L M N O P Q

R S T U V W X Y Z

a b c d e f g h i j k l m

n o p q r s t u v w x y z

1 2 3 4 5 6 7 8 9 0

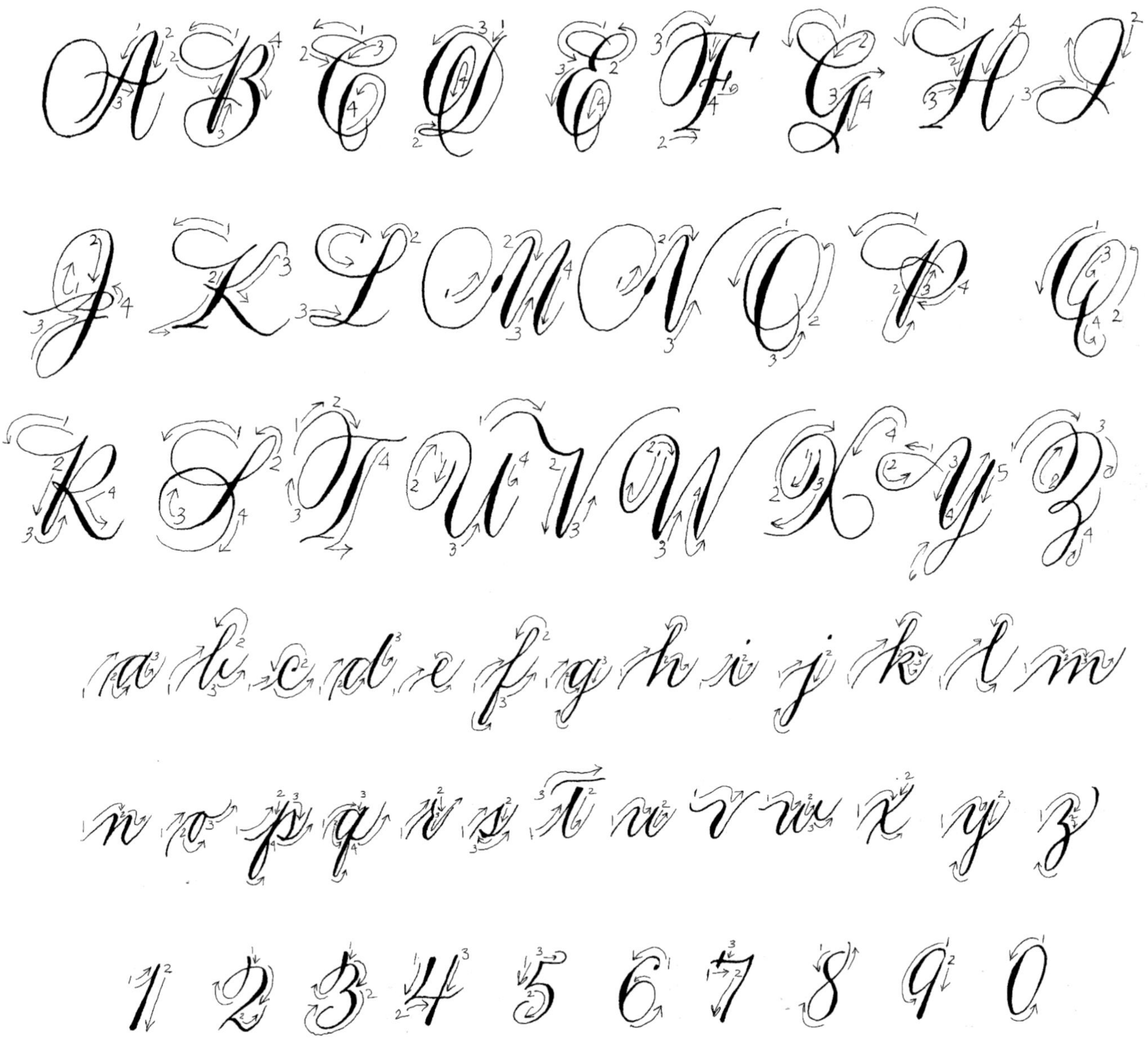
A B C D E F G H I
J K L M N O P Q
R S T U V W X Y Z
a b c d e f g h i j k l m
n o p q r s t u v w x y z
1 2 3 4 5 6 7 8 9 0

scroll INVITATION

An unusual and unique way to present a wedding invitation, the scroll automatically conjures up images of medieval proclamations and Renaissance feasts, town criers, nobility at court, and all of Shakespeare's romantic characters. The soft, mottled surface of today's parchment is perfectly suited for this project. Despite its slight translucence, it is very strong. Using a flourished, Italic hand for the text adds to the historic aura and romance of the document. A contrasting paper or paper-backed fabric set behind the parchment creates contrast for the mailed invitation, which is rolled into a scroll, tied with ribbon, and inserted into a mailing tube. It is difficult to write directly onto a cylinder, so use good-quality mailing labels to address each tube.

MATERIALS

- parchment paper
- paper-backed brocade fabric
- organza ribbon—12" (30 cm per invitation)
- mailing tube
- labels
- broad-edged calligraphy pens
- black ink
- pencil
- soft eraser
- computer
- light box
- for variation: gold ink

Because you have shared in our lives
by your friendship and love
you are invited to share with us...

Sarah Lynn Chambers

and

Michael James Foss

When we exchange marriage vows
and begin our new life together
on Saturday, the ninth of June
two thousand and one
at half past two o'clock in the afternoon
Clairmont Country Club
Clairmont, Maryland

Reception immediately following ceremony **1**

CALLIGRAPHER BEVERLY WLADKOWSKI

TIPS AND TECHNIQUES

• If you do not have a computer, draft the text with pencil on paper that is the same size as the finished invitation. Write over the pencil draft quickly with pen to help decide spacing. Cut the draft into separate lines; then paste or tape the lines onto another sheet of the same size to center the text. Use this as the master draft.

• Although a light box makes this project easier, it is not completely necessary. Set the text of the computerized document in a very heavy type if a light box is not available. Parchment paper is somewhat translucent, so the bold image from the computer printout should show through.

• Check with your local Post Office to see if there are any special requirements for mailing tubes, such as the required size and method of wrapping or sealing the tube.

• The brocade fabric shown here is backed with paper and was purchased as an 8 1/2" x 11" (22 cm x 28 cm) sheet in a specialty paper store.

2

3

STEP 1 Using a computer, type the invitation text into a document. Set margins to make it the same size as the finished invitation. Center the text and add line breaks. Use fonts similar in size and spacing to the calligraphic alphabet for the finished product. This layout may require several drafts to get it right.

STEP 2 Place the computer printout on your light box and a piece of parchment paper on top of it, so the printout can be seen through the parchment. Follow the size and placement of the computer type as a guide for lettering the invitation onto the parchment. Lightly pencil-in the names of the bride and groom matching the shapes of the calligraphic letters.

STEP 3 Begin to write the text portion of the invitation in ink. Omit the names of the bride and groom but ink the "and" between them. When the text is dry, use a larger nib on the calligraphy pen to add the couple's names. Allow to dry thoroughly. Carefully erase the pencil guides.

VARIATION For an extra decorative touch, write the names of the bride and groom in gold ink.

guest table NAMES

One of today's popular wedding trends is to assign a name, rather than a number, to each reception table as a means of informing guests of their seating assignments. Tables can be named after cities where the couple has vacationed, hobbies or interests, romantic song titles, or, as presented here, words relating to love and marriage. In addition to the table name, include a few thoughts, a poem, or a quotation related to the word's theme. Place the table name in a beautiful frame worthy of display throughout the reception.

MATERIALS

- picture frames with freestanding easel back
- watercolor paper
- watercolor paint
- pencil
- fine-tipped calligraphy pen
- black ink
- soft eraser

ETIQUETTE ADVICE

It may be more difficult for guests to find their seats when tables are identified with names instead of numbers, especially at a large wedding with many tables. Consider providing a calligraphic map next to the escort cards, showing the location of each table name in the room. Alternatively, ask an usher, bridesmaid, or member of the catering staff to stand near the entrance and direct guests to the correct area in the room.

1

- Flowers can be painted to sit behind the text or to frame it around the borders. If planning to render text over a painting, be sure that the text is legible.

- Watercolor paper has a soft, giving finish that erases cleanly. Be gentle when erasing so as not to damage the paper's surface or smudge the illustration or lettering.

2

STEP 1 Measure and cut the watercolor paper to fit the frame. Paint a flower in the center of the card using watercolor paint or calligraphy ink.

STEP 2 When the watercolor paint is completely dry, add rules as guides for sizing the letters. Draft text in pencil to work out the spacing.

STEP 3 Render the text using a fine-tipped calligraphy pen and black ink. Let the ink dry thoroughly before erasing pencil marks.

3

VARIATION In addition to changing the name of each table, paint a different flower on each card to add visual interest. Any favorite flowers can be applied, or choose flowers that coordinate with those used in the centerpieces.

combination
PLACE CARDS

MATERIALS

for unadorned place cards:

• purchased place cards

• black ink

• fine-tipped calligraphy pen

• broad-edged calligraphy pen

for burgundy place cards:

• purchased place cards

• gold paper

• gold ink

• fine-tipped calligraphy pen

• broad-edged calligraphy pen

• decorative hole punch

• glue stick

for flower-studded place card:

• purchased place cards

• black or colored ink

• silk flower bud (or watercolor paint and fine paintbrush)

• fine-tipped calligraphy pen

• broad-edged calligraphy pen

• glue gun

for ribboned place card:

• purchased place cards

• blue ink

• 6" (15 cm) of ribbon per card

• fine-tipped calligraphy pen

• broad-edged calligraphy pen

for variaton:

• purchased place cards

• black ink

• fine-tipped calligraphy pen

• broad-edged calligraphy pen

Place cards, also known as escort cards, are used to indicate a guest's seating assignment. They are often the first detail encountered when entering a wedding reception. Beautiful calligraphy adds a touch of romance to any card. The combination of writing the first name in a fine-tipped Copperplate script at a jaunty angle and writing the last name with a block print using a broad-edged Italic nib gives the card further interest. Cards can be purchased in various colors and sizes.

VERSION 1 Gold ink adds dramatic interest to a burgundy place card. Use a decorative hole punch to tie the cards to a theme or season. Back the decoratively punched card with a small piece of paper in a contrasting color or one that coordinates with the ink color. Adhere with a glue stick. Alternatively, attach the cutouts to the card, allowing them to extend over the top of the fold.

TIPS AND TECHNIQUES

• Tent cards are available prepackaged in office supply and stationery stores or can be ordered to match other wedding stationery items. Any fine quality, heavyweight paper that will hold ink well can be cut to size and folded to make handmade cards.

• Ribbons come in every size, color, and fabric you can imagine. Organza, tulle, silk, and satin are particularly romantic. French wired ribbons will hold any shape they are placed in, while ribbons without wires have a natural bounce when tied into a bow.

VERSION 2 A delicate flower painted onto a place card adds grace and beauty. As an alternative, attach a three-dimensional bud using a silk or dried flower. Adhere with hot glue.

VERSION 3 Anchor a beautiful bow by punching two holes close together in the upper left corner of the card. Choose a wide ribbon for a lavish effect or a narrower ribbon for a more tailored look. The long tails of the ribbon create a veil over the guest's name. Colors can coordinate or contrast.

VARIATION Practice makes perfect, and a practiced hand can embellish a card with pen alone. Elaborate flourishes complement the script lettering and need no additional decoration.

menu CARD

Whether the meal is a luncheon buffet or a sit-down dinner, telling the guests what is being served is always appreciated. Menu cards can be displayed on the table the same way that table numbers are, or a menu can be placed at each table setting. Lettered with beautiful script, the cards are beautiful on their own. To embellish them even more, add a painted flower, or wrap the card in a beautiful tissue and finish with a bow.

MATERIALS

- white paper
- card stock
- art tissue
- ribbon for bow
- watercolor paint
- black ink
- fine paintbrush
- fine-tipped calligraphy pen
- tape
- light box
- computer with scanner
- for variation: petal paper

Mixed Green Salad with Vegetables
Cold Poached Salmon with Dill Sauce
Orange Roughy with Buerre Blanc Sauce
Sliced Roast Beef with Rosemary au Jus and Horseradish Sauce
Oven Roasted Turkey Breast with Cranberry Chutney
Chicken Cacciatore

1

TIPS AND TECHNIQUES

• Long lines of text can be difficult to render in a straight line. Adding rules to indicate the baseline and waist-line will help guide your hand as well as keep track of the x-height for the letters.

• Adding dingbats, or small, decorative ornaments, between the menu sections helps to visually break up text and organize the menu elements into courses or food groups.

Mixed Green Salad with Vegetables

Cold Poached Salmon with Dill Sauce
Orange Roughy with Buerre Blanc Sauce
Sliced Roast Beef with Rosemary au Jus and Horseradish Sauce

2

Mixed Green Salad with Vegetables

Cold Poached Salmon with Dill Sauce
Orange Roughy with Buerre Blanc Sauce
Sliced Roast Beef with Rosemary au Jus and Horseradish Sauce
Oven Roasted Turkey Breast with Cranberry Chutney
Chicken Cacciatore
Sauteed Chicken Marsala

Choice of Penne, Rigatoni or Farfalle Pasta
with Vodka, Marinara or Bolognase Sauce

Double Baked Potatoes
Wild Rice
Haricots Verts Bundles
Assorted Crusty Breads and Rolls

Viennese Dessert Table
Ice Cream Sundae Bar
Wedding Cake
Coffee and Tea Service

3

STEP 1 Create a draft for the text on a computer using a typeface similar in size and spacing to the lettering style you have chosen. Add rules to use as guidelines for each line.

STEP 2 Placing the draft on a light box and the white paper on top, render the text. Adjust the horizontal and vertical layout by cutting the text and taping it to the card stock in proper alignment to create a mechanical.

STEP 3 Scan the mechanical, clean up the edges and tape marks, and print the menu on card stock.

VARIATION An interesting method of displaying the menu is to roll it around each guest's napkin like a napkin ring. Use petal paper or vellum to match the colors used throughout the room.

CALLIGRAPHERS
SUSAN L. RAMSEY
CHRISTOPHER J. WATKINS
HILARY WILLIAMS

a fine ROMANCE

A wedding oozes romance. This is not the time to be shy about showing emotion. What does "romance" mean to you? Is it soft, sentimental, nostalgic, sweet? How would that feeling translate into something more tangible? Here are a few ideas to consider.

For starters, choose a lettering style that fits the bill. The more ornate, the more romantic it is. The passionately flourished capitals, ascenders, and descenders of pointed-pen scripts connect and intertwine, mimicking the joining of two lives and families. But don't ignore the broad-edged pen alphabets. The sweeping swashes of a flourished Italic are as romantic as any Copperplate and bring to mind the grace of Renaissance times.

Incorporate passages of romantic poetry into the invitation or menu. Add love quotes to place cards. Name the tables after famous couples. Inscribe romantic passages in beautiful calligraphy on place mats, table runners, or napkin rings made of exquisite paper.

Sophistication and elegance are always romantic, yet tasteful adornment can add to the effect. Ribbon is a simple complement that packs a romantic wallop. Tie together more than one for a multicolored bow, or tie the ends into a cluster of love knots. Weave ribbons into a patchwork for your program cover or to decorate the place card table. Wrap your invitation in lace or brocade, or create ruffles of organza, tulle, satin, or luscious silk to adorn almost anything. A table full of favors wrapped in sumptuous fabrics with tags of sweeping calligraphy creates a romantic display.

Flowers are romantic in any form and can be incorporated in many ways. Add a delicate, fresh blossom to place cards, a handful of dried lavender to invitation envelopes, or a garland painted with watercolor to adorn your envelopes.

Use color judiciously for a whisper of romance. A touch of gold, opulent and regal, enriches lettering or materials. Pastel colors murmur and blush, adding a suggestion of endearment.

Finally, find a way to make it personal. Incorporate family traditions into the wedding details. Display wedding photos of family members with a sign rendered in beautiful script explaining who's who. Create a calligraphic family tree or timeline of the couple's lives. Giving guests even a hint of the intimate affection shared by bride and groom will pull on each and every heartstring.

By all means, use discretion. Don't overdo any of these ideas, as too much of a good thing will definitely push your work beyond the limits of good taste.

• Seal the envelopes with sealing wax.

• Add a hint of perfume to the invitation.

• Buy the beautiful "Love" postage stamps for mailing invitations.

• Place the guest book on a bed of rose petals.

Modern

Please join us for a
Post Wedding Brunch
Sunday, November twenty-third at twelve noon
at the home of

Chen and Alexandra Tse

103 Fifth Avenue

Apartment 801

Regrets only

212-555-7463

W&A 5·2·01

& Sparks invite you to witness
the marriage of their daughter

Peter Lincoln Holbrook

the sixth of September
afternoon

modern CALLIGRAPHY

In the twentieth century, mass-produced, printed matter became cost efficient. Consequently, new typefaces were being developed constantly. With the advent of the personal computer, handwriting practically became obsolete. Classic, elegant, romantic, and artistic—these words easily can be used to categorize the calligraphic form. Applying the word "modern" almost seems like an anomaly. Yet, in the grand scheme of calligraphy's history, alphabets developed to copy twentieth-century typefaces can certainly be considered modern.

The art of letters has come full circle. Each generation looks to the past, selectively choosing styles that are appealing and adapting them to modern sensibilities. Traditional form becomes updated. In today's world, there is a whole new breed of weddings, and you can successfully pair a calligraphic style with your forward-thinking attitude. The modern Italic shown here is an updated version of the classic, while the French Rondo is based on a typeface in wide use today. Clean lines, interesting materials, bold colors, and progressive design all contribute to overall appearance, updating calligraphy for the twenty-first century wedding.

Searching for a lettering style for one of her own invitations, this calligrapher used an invitation she found in a magazine as a jumping-off point and developed this unique, modern, Italic hand. Although it has a distinct "brush" quality, it is created with a broad-edged pen and many pen twists, particularly on the exit strokes of the letters. To attain the finest hairlines, she drags a bit of wet ink with one corner of her pen nib.

CALLIGRAPHER MELISSA DINWIDDIE

A B C D E F G H
I J K L M N O P Q
R S T U V W X Y Z
a b c d e f g h i j k l m
n o p q r s t u v w x y z
1 2 3 4 5 6 7 8 9 0

ABCDEFGH
IJKLMNOPQ
RSTUVWXYZ
abcdefghijklm
nopqrstuvwxyz
1234567890

Sweet and charming without being overly fussy or outdated, this nostalgic style shows us that everything old can be new again. Its clean lines are similar to some of today's most popular typefaces. Created with a broad-edged pen, the round, vertical letters of this uncluttered alphabet gives a modern interpretation of the seventeenth-century Ronde style. CALLIGRAPHER LISA J. KENNEDY

A B C D E F G H
I J K L M N O P Q
R S T U V W X Y Z
a b c d e f g h i j k l m
n o p q r s t u v w x y z
1 2 3 4 5 6 7 8 9 0

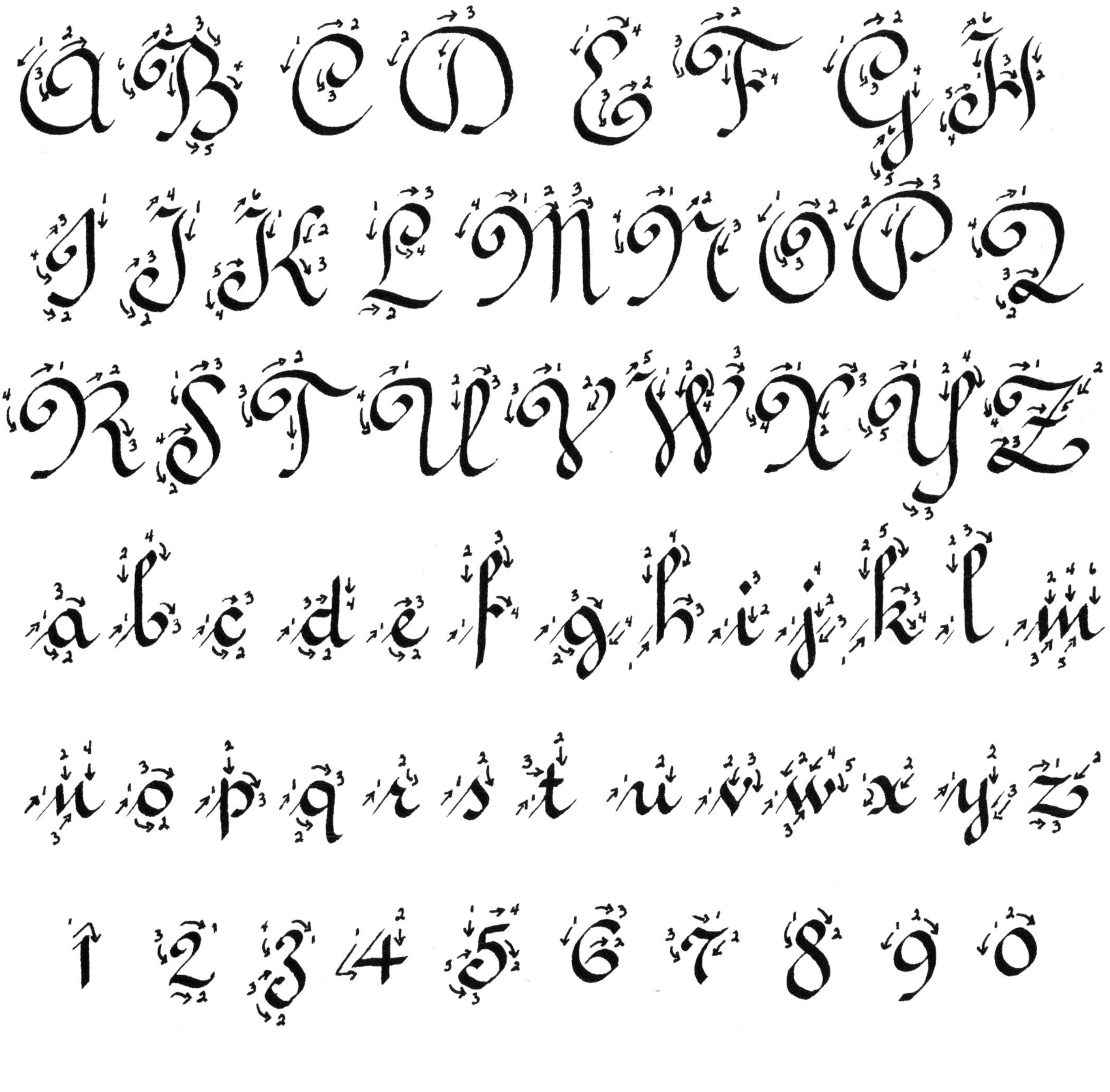

initial TAGS

Favors are a charming way to thank guests for attending the wedding. Bags made of hand-made paper and silver skeleton leaves are a fun and simple way to package your favors. Decorating with handmade tags adds a nice personal touch. The tags here show the bride's and groom's first initials rendered in the modern Italic alphabet along with the wedding date. The couple's new monogram would be a lovely alternative. The tag is attached with a coordinating silver organza ribbon threaded through two holes in the top of the bag and tied into a lively bow. Place them directly on the tables at each place setting.

MATERIALS

- white paper
- watercolor paper
- purchased favor bags
- 2" (5 cm) wide organza ribbon—18" (46 cm) long per bag
- broad-edged calligraphy pen
- black ink
- computer with scanner
- scissors
- hole punch
- for variation: pinking shears or decorative-edge scissors

ETIQUETTE ADVICE

Favors can be placed at each setting on the table, hand-ed to guests at any point during the reception, or left at the door for them to take on their way out. Although it may seem obvious that the gift is meant for the guest, when leaving favors unattended, provide a sign or incorporate the information into the tag to eliminate any ambiguity.

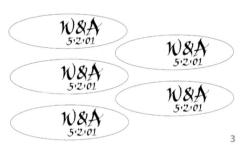

1

- Use a photocopier instead of a scanner to enlarge or reduce the size of the mechanical and duplicate the tags en masse.

STEP 1 Render the text to create a mechanical, using a broad-edged calligraphy pen and black ink.

STEP 2 Scan the text into a computer layout program and try it in different configurations, altering the size and placement of the text as well as the shape of the tag. Cut the tags out and test them with the favor bag to find the most pleasing arrangement.

STEP 3 Duplicate the chosen tag in the document. Then print out as many as needed on watercolor paper. Cut them out, and punch a hole at one end for the ribbon.

2

3

VARIATION Choose a petal paper bag and a colored ribbon to incorporate wedding colors into the favors. Experiment with pinking shears or decorative-edged scissors when cutting out the tags.

w e d d i n g   INVITATION

While there will always be a demand for the classic, understated wedding invitation, it does not suit everyone. For the cutting-edge bride and groom, an invitation that reflects personal style, as well as the style of the event, is more appropriate. It is not necessary to forfeit good taste, as this modern invitation clearly shows. Beautiful calligraphy paired with a speckled card stock maintains the elegance of the document, while the bold paper used to wrap the invitation updates it for the new millennium. A delicate art tissue is affixed to the colored paper with spray mount, and raffia is used to keep the outer wrapping closed.

MATERIALS

• white paper or grid paper

• colored art paper to wrap invitation

• art tissue

• raffia

• black ink

• broad-edged calligraphy pen

• spray mount

• for variation: colored art tissue, white satin ribbon

1

2

3

- It can be easier to write the text in a different size than the finished work. Most printing methods can decrease or enlarge the size of an original to meet specifications.

- Feel free to play with the proportion and placement of the text. Here, the names of the bride and groom were enlarged for the mechanical more than the original rendering.

- Spray mount has a tendency to spread and leave a sticky residue. Protect your work surfaces with newspaper, or do all the spraying inside a large cardboard box. Work in a well-ventilated area.

STEP 1 Render the text at a comfortable working size on graph paper. Using a photocopier, experiment with the size of the text. Move lines of type around to test different arrangements.

STEP 2 Once the proportion of the type is determined, cut and paste the individual lines to create a centered mechanical, and determine the final size to which the mechanical will be reduced. For this invitation, the mechanical was reduced by 65 percent.

STEP 3 Choose the paper stock and printing method. Scan, print, and cut the invitations, or have it done by a professional printer.

VARIATION A softer version of the same design uses a pale blue, translucent art tissue to wrap the invitation, allowing the invitation to be seen through its wrapping. A white satin bow replaces the raffia.

CALLIGRAPHER MELISSA DINWIDDIE
CRAFT ARTIST BETTE MATTHEWS

postwedding brunch
INVITATION

When the party is over, don't roll up the red carpet right away. Many newlyweds host a casual gathering the day after the wedding for family members, close friends, and out-of-town guests. When designing an invitation for this, let your personal style rule. This line of basic cards and self-mailer envelopes can be purchased in many colors and sizes. You can also make them yourself with card stock. The card shown is personalized with handmade paper and some torn metallic tissue. The invitation is printed on transparency film. The envelopes can be sealed with a sticker or a sealing wax stamp using your new monogram.

MATERIALS

- white paper or grid paper
- metallic art tissue
- handmade paper
- printable transparency film
- 5" x 5" (13 cm x 13 cm) card
- 8" x 8" (20 cm x 20 cm) mailer
- 1/8" (3 mm) wide satin ribbon
- black ink
- broad-edged calligraphy pen
- light box
- white craft glue
- computer with scanner
- for variation: colored art tissue, white satin ribbon

ETIQUETTE ADVICE

Invitations to casual, next day events can be mailed several weeks in advance or handed to the guest at the wedding. Without advance notice, however, guests may not be available to join you.

Please join us for a
Post-Wedding Brunch
Sunday, November twenty-third at twelve noon
at the home of
Chen and Alexandra Tse
103 Fifth Avenue
Apartment 801

Regrets only
212-555-7463

1

Please

Post - We

2

TIPS AND TECHNIQUES

- Transparency film will show fingerprints, so hold it only around the edges. Cover with a piece of paper or tissue when cutting it.

- If you don't have a light box, make the lines on the grid heavy enough to be seen through the paper on which you are rendering.

- As an alternative to ribbon, attach the layers of paper and transparency film with stickers or sealing wax.

STEP 1 Render a draft of the invitation on a grid to work out the spacing. Work at a comfortable size; the text can be reduced to the final size with the computer. Measure each line, and mark the length of the line in a centered position on the grid.

STEP 2 Place white paper on top of the grid set on a light box. Render the final text. If necessary, also use the draft rendering as a guide. Scan the text into the computer and clean up any smudges.

STEP 3 Print the invitation onto transparency film. (You should be able to fit two invitations onto one sheet of film.) Cut out the 5" x 5" (13 cm x 13 cm) invitation from the film. Tear the handmade paper into an interesting shape and glue it to the 5" x 5" (13 cm x 13 cm) base card. Tear the metallic tissue into small pieces and glue it to the handmade paper. Assemble all pieces and punch two small holes through all layers at the top.

VARIATION There are endless combinations of colors and materials that can be used to change the look of this invitation. Here, the taxi-cab yellow mailer matches the top layer of the card, onto which the invitation was printed directly. A piece of checkered tissue is layered over the top, and a bronze card adds contrast to the border.

Artistic

Ashley
& Scott

Elizabe

You're invited to a
Bridesmaids' Tea
Thursday, the fourteenth of April
at four o'clock in the afternoon
Salon de Te
74 Oakhill Drive
Reply to Bridget

artistic CALLIGRAPHY

Calligraphy today is an art form on a different level. It is no longer used as the sole means of preserving ideas in books or as the preferred method of communication among societal elite. Instead, it has become a means to convey something distinctive, something personal, in both correspondence and in art. Today's calligraphers have the freedom to express themselves in almost any way they see fit. So when it comes to designing scripts for a wedding, choosing between a classic format or a modern one doesn't have to limit the level of imagination you can bring to it.

In this chapter, two alphabets are presented. Each uses a different pen. Each demonstrates the liberties that can be applied to traditional letterforms to shape a personalized vision. Combined with art, unusual formats, and attention-grabbing materials, calligraphy can be used to transform the typical into the exceptional. The four projects in this chapter give added oomph to common, wedding-related details. In addition to the ideas offered here, look through favorite magazines for typefaces and objects of interest. Then consider how to translate them to the many decorative details of your wedding. With artistic projects, the sky is the limit.

CALLIGRAPHER CHRISTOPHER J. WATKINS

This alphabet was developed by the calligrapher as a counterpoint to the rigid tendencies of classic calligraphy. In search of something loose and upbeat, he created this rock-and-roll lettering style called Hollywood. Render this alphabet with a pointed pen keeping your hand free and loose. The letters shown are offered as a guide. Add extra flourishes if the page needs to be balanced, or tone down the letters if one area is overemphasized.

CALLIGRAPHER CHRISTOPHER J. WATKINS

A B C D E F G H
I J K L M N O P Q
R S T U V W X Y Z
a b or b c d or d e f g h i j k l m or m
n or n o p g r or r s or s t u v w x y z
1 2 3 4 5 6 7 8 9 0

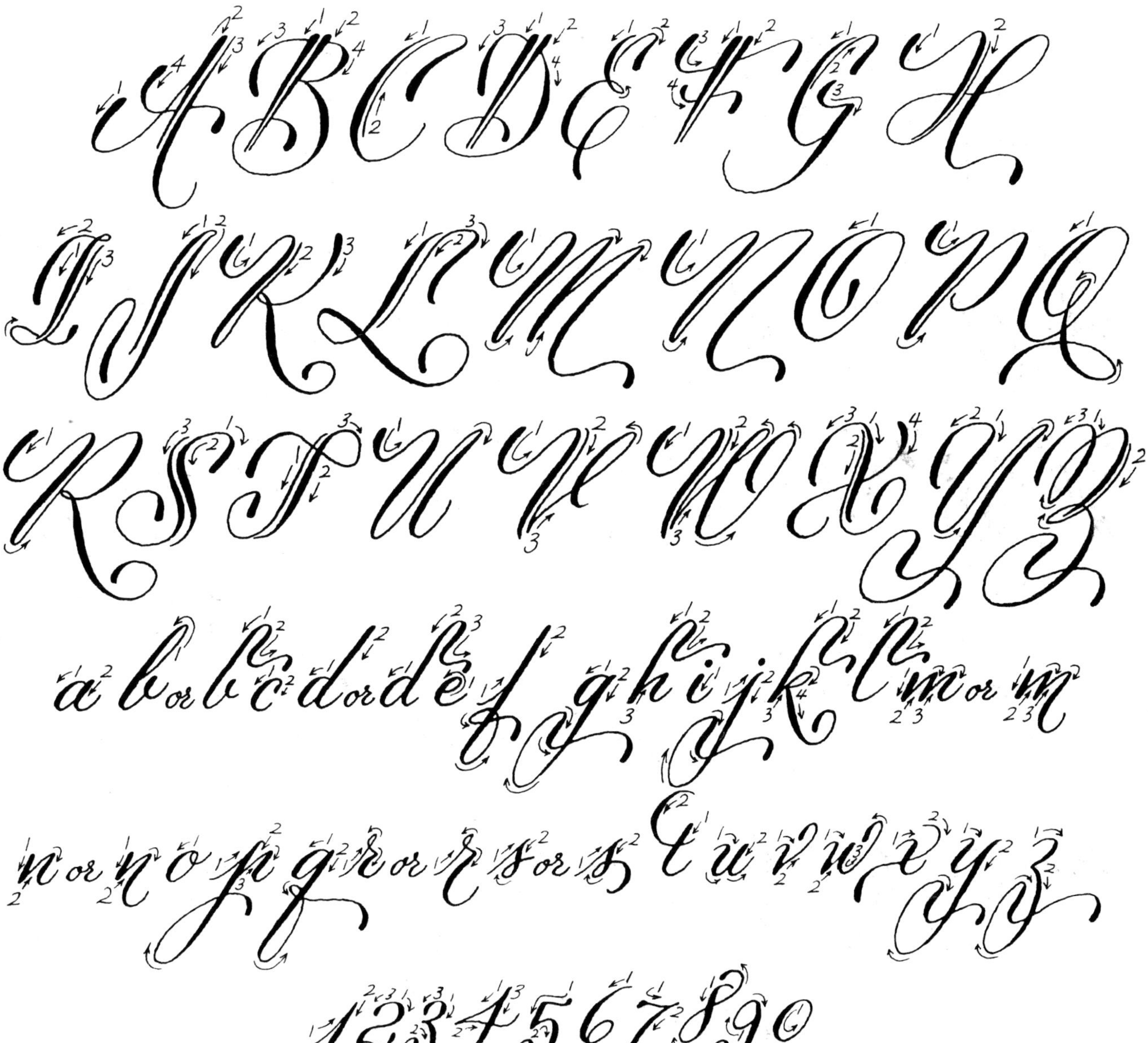

Tired of the tightly designed hands typically used in classic calligraphy, this lettering artist put some fun in his form. The letters are based on an alphabet he originally produced for a client's invitation to a full-scale Texas barbecue. Fondly dubbed "Will Rogers," this style is written with a broad-edged calligraphy pen and based on traditional, upright calligraphy forms. Departing from the stiff structure of the model letters, the impression it leaves is sweet and warm and not at all rigid. CALLIGRAPHER CHRISTOPHER J. WATKINS

A B C D E F G H
I J K L M N O P Q
R S T U V W X Y Z
a b c d e f g h i j k l m
n o p q r or r s or s t u v w x y z
1 2 3 4 5 6 7 8 9 0

ABCDEFGH
IJKLMNOPQ
RSTUVWXYZ
abcdefghijklm
nopqr or r s or s tuvwxyz
1234567890

bridesmaids' tea
INVITATION

A bride often hosts a party for her bridesmaids shortly before the wedding to thank them for the support they have given her throughout the planning process. This event may take the form of a luncheon, a sleepover, or one of the most charming gatherings—tea. The purpose of the invitation is not just to communicate what, where, when, and who, but to entice guests with a taste of the upcoming festivities. Because you do not have to make up dozens of invitations for this event, each can be created by hand. Here the invitation is folded into thirds and opens vertically. For a finishing touch, it is held shut with a demure bow.

MATERIALS

- white paper
- lavender card stock
- 1/8" (3 mm) wide satin ribbon—two 32" (81 cm) lengths per invitation
- colored pencils
- fine-tipped calligraphy pen
- permanent black ink
- light box
- table knife
- ruler
- fine paintbrush
- glue gun
- for variation: teapot rubber stamp, purple ink pad

ETIQUETTE ADVICE

For an intimate event such as this, the name of the location and street address of the event should be all that is needed. If the guests are all close friends or family members, it is unnecessary for the bride to include her telephone number with the R.s.v.p.

1

TIPS AND TECHNIQUES

• When cutting paper stock for a custom-designed invitation, choose the envelope first. Cut the stock at least 1/8" (3 mm) smaller than the envelope for ease of insertion.

• If the folding front panels of the card are not the same size, be sure to keep the orientation of the paper correct, or you may create your work upside down.

• Use a photograph of a teacup or teapot from a magazine as an inspiration for the cover design by tracing the outline and copying the colors.

2

3

STEP 1 On two sheets of white paper measure a working area that is the size of the invitation. On one sheet, sketch the cover design. On the other, rule the text area and draft the text in pencil to center the spacing. When the text looks centered, render it in ink to create a template.

STEP 2 Cut the card stock to size, adding a 1-inch (3 cm) margin on all sides. Allow for 2 inches (5 cm) of overlap on the front panels. Lay the card stock over the templates on a light box and trace the teacup design on one side of the sheet in ink and the lettering on the other side with a calligraphy pen.

STEP 3 Enhance the cover design with colored pencils. On the outside of the invitation, score the fold lines using a dull table knife and ruler. With a fine brush, paint a line of water along one of the 1" (3 cm) borders of the invitation, then fold back and forth along the line until the crease seems to set. Tear the border gently along the crease to create a deckled edge to the paper. Repeat on the other three sides. Using a hot glue gun, attach the ribbon to the back of the invitation at the center and the outer edges.

VARIATION Rubber stamps come in a delightful assortment of designs and eliminate the need to create a graphic image from scratch. Choose a stamp appropriate to the theme of the party. Use colorful ink and fill in the pattern with colored pencils.

guest BOOK

At the wedding itself, guests are filled with the joy of the day and warm wishes for the couple. Create a stunning book where guests can record their sentiments during the reception. The book can be left at the entrance door near the place cards or on the gift table. Alternatively, ask an attendant to take it around to each table. Dazzling books such as this can be purchased and personalized by inscribing the pages and cover. The handmade paper for this book's cover is a poor surface for calligraphy ink, so the text was penned on a separate sheet of paper, which was mounted to a card in a coordinating color. Both pieces were then bonded to the front with white craft glue. A ribbon was glued around the border to finish the edges.

MATERIALS

• purchased guest book, photo album, or scrapbook

• colored card stock

• colored paper

• ribbon

• black ink

• green ink

• magenta ink

• broad-edged calligraphy pen with different sized nibs

• fine-tipped pen

• ruler

• white craft glue

• computer

• for variation: self-adhesive photo corners

1

- Test the paper inside a book to see if you can safely apply ink to the surface. A small dot placed on the last page of the book should suffice and will hardly be noticed.

- If your ink begins to spread and bleed, try a different ink. You can also cover the page with three or four light coats of spray fixative and test again.

- If all else fails, purchase suitable paper and glue it directly to the book pages. This can also be a great timesaving device: create one page, scan it into the computer, and print enough pages for the entire book.

2

STEP 1 In a computer layout program, or by hand, create a template for the page in black ink. Make sure all the type and lines are thick and can be seen through the pages in the book. If the book's pages are thick with no transparency, use a pencil to draft the layout directly on the book page.

STEP 2 With the broad-edged pens, begin inking the text in the open book. Add visual interest by using different sized pen nibs to write the words in different sizes and colored inks that match the book or wedding colors.

STEP 3 With a fine-tipped pen and ruler, add straight lines to the page to indicate where the guest should wri

3

VARIATION Polaroid photographs are a popular modern addition to this tradition. Encourage guests to photograph themselves and place the photo on the page with their remarks. Self-adhesive photo corners make the process easy.

CALLIGRAPHER CHRISTOPHER J. WATKINS
CRAFT ARTIST BETTE MATTHEWS

jazz and PIZZAZZ

Many works of art utilizing calligraphy are created on canvas, glass, ceramics, and textiles, as well as on paper. Imagination, technique, arrangement, and execution all combine for a visual performance. There are many ways to add that extra bit of animation to a more practical work, such as a wedding invitation. Certainly, when it comes to keepsakes, the sky is the limit.

IT'S ALL IN THE ALPHABET

Any of the alphabets in this book can be made more artistic with a few well-placed flourishes. Review the projects that use swashes and swirls in each of the chapters, and determine what appeals to you—and what doesn't! On a practice sheet, try applying "embroidery" to your favorite alphabet. Create large initial caps on the first letters of words or names you want to highlight. Then add color, delicate painted flowers, or birds, or engulf them in swirls of gold and silver.

Experiment! Elongate capital letters. Take a classic typeface and widen the letters till they are full and round. Let your characters dance along a wavy line instead of lining up horizontally. Turn your handwriting into a lettering style. The result will be something unique.

MATERIAL MATTERS

Take it one step further by incorporating material embellishments. A stroll through a fine paper, art supply, or crafts store will present so many sumptuous materials that the problem will be in choosing just one. Add a handmade paper to your project, or make your own. Mail your invitation in a vellum envelope. Pair paper and fabric. Use art tissue to add depth and dimension. Create layers of materials to border and frame the text. Add hand-painted illustrations, clip art, or photography. There are many craft supplies that can be tastefully applied to your wedding projects: rubber stamps, embossing powder, pressed or dried flowers.

Use the element of surprise. Pair a classic typeface with a daring design or color. Don't be afraid that it isn't "wedding-ish." These days, almost anything goes. Color, texture, contrast, and design should all be considered when planning your work. Be bold. Make a statement. Or be demure or delicate. Whatever suits your style. Keep in mind one rule of thumb—embellishment should add to a piece, not overwhelm or obscure it—and let your imagination soar.

QUICK TIPS

• Once you have designed the lettering, take a step back and review the overall impression of the page. Does an area look unfinished or blank? This is the perfect place for an artistic addition.

• Don't overdo it! Too much embellishment loses its impact and the piece becomes boring or even illegible.

wedding etiquette
FOR BRIDES

In the casual atmosphere we live in today, we don't often think about etiquette. Yet, when it comes to anything wedding related, knowing and using the conventions of etiquette can be an invaluable tool to guide you through the many rituals.

Rules of etiquette must be combined with your own judgement at times. Although referred to as "rules" they are really principles to steer you in the direction of civility and thoughtfulness, and sometimes must be adapted to suit your particular circumstances. Different customs apply in different areas of the country and the world, and traditions vary in families and diverse cultural backgrounds. Even the experts have different opinions on certain points. There are many, many points and nuances of wedding etiquette—more than can possibly be listed in these few pages. I encourage you to purchase a book devoted to the subject for more in-depth advice. The following merely touches on matters of etiquette related to the written elements of a wedding.

GIFTS AND REGISTRIES

The registry is a wish list. It is there to help guide those that require guidance. Guests are not obligated to purchase gifts from your registry. Choose items in a wide range of prices and styles to suit your own taste, allowing the gift giver greater variety of selections. It is inappropriate to list registry information, or any mention of gifts, on any invitation or announcement other than a bridal shower invitation. Gifts should not be expected for your engagement or engagement party. If any are given, they should be promptly acknowledged with a handwritten thank you note. Gifts should not be opened at any large event except for the bridal shower. Sometimes the bride and groom would prefer to receive money rather than gifts. It is inappropriate for them to indicate this. The polite way to inform people of this option is to mention it to your closest family members or intimate friends. Then they can properly pass on your wishes to anyone that asks.

THANK YOU NOTES

There is some confusion regarding the "one-year rule" surrounding wedding gifts. A person is within the boundaries of traditional etiquette to send a gift to the bride and groom any time up until their first anniversary. Under no circumstances is this freedom extended to the couple in terms of responding. Every gift you are given—engagement, shower, wedding, etc.—must be acknowledged promptly with its own handwritten note of thanks. "Promptly" is defined, in this case, as within two weeks for a gift received prior to the wedding and within one month for a gift received at the event or shortly thereafter. Some experts grant a grace period of up to three months for gifts received at or immediately after the wedding. The idea is to write your thank you notes as soon as possible. Each note should be personal, though it doesn't have to be long. It should mention the gift given and make some statement about how appreciative you are of the gift itself or the thought that went into choosing it. For gifts of money, indicate how you intend to use it. Under no circumstances is a form letter acceptable.

CALLIGRAPHER ANGELA R. WELCH/PEN AND PAUPER

Mr. and Mrs. Nicholas Carroll
145 Dearborn Street
Chicago, Illinois 60623

Mr. and Mrs. Nicholas Carroll
145 Dearborn Street
Chicago, Illinois 60623

Mr. and Mrs. Nicholas Carroll
145 Dearborn Street
Chicago, Illinois 60623

A printed card can be used for the outside of your note, as long as your personal thanks are written inside.

BRIDAL SHOWER

The shower should be held anywhere from two weeks to two months before the wedding. Anyone may host a shower for the bride. This responsibility most often falls to the maid of honor and/or bridesmaids. Strictly speaking, members of the bride's immediate family are not supposed to host a shower as it might be seen as blatant solicitation of gifts. The exception would be if a bride chooses a member of her family as an honor attendant or if there is no other candidate to host the shower. Shower guests are usually close friends and relations and only those who will be invited to the wedding. There are two exceptions. If the wedding itself is very small, a large shower may take the place of a reception, and anyone close the bride or her family can be invited. Second, coworkers often give the bride a shower in the office, without any expectation that they will be invited to the wedding. The host of the party always decides on the number of guests.

BRIDESMAIDS' PARTY

To thank her attendants for the help and support they have given during the planning process and on the day of the wedding, the bride often hosts a party in their honor. It is a wonderful time to distribute gifts of thanks. This generally happens in the week or two preceding the wedding. If some attendants are not located in your area, schedule this event the day before the wedding or even as a luncheon on the day of an evening wedding. It can be a delightful "time out" in the hectic days just before the event.

INVITATIONS

See page 34.

OUTER ENVELOPES

Do not use abbreviations, except "Mr." or "Mrs." or "Dr.," if you choose. Use the abbreviation "Ms." if you think it's appropriate. All names should be spelled in full. If you intend to include it, the middle name should be spelled out as well. Words such as "Avenue" and "Street" should be spelled out, as should the state. It is acceptable to use numerals in the street address. Married couples with different last names or unmarried couples living together receive one invitation with both of their names listed on two separate lines. Ideally, children over the age of thirteen should receive their own invitation. If young children are invited, their names are not included on the outer envelope, unless you are not using inner envelopes. In this case, the child's name should be listed on a separate line underneath the parents' names. If inviting a single person to bring a date, the most formal procedure would be to find out the name of the date and send a separate invitation to the person. However, it is much more common to send one invitation to the person that you know and to indicate on the inner envelope that a date is welcome. It is ideal to specify the person's name if you can find it out. If not, it is acceptable to write "and Guest" after your friend's name on the inner envelope. The outer envelope should be addressed to your friend only, unless the date is someone you know or the couple's relationship is serious. If not using inner envelopes, include a handwritten note inviting your friend to bring someone. A return address should be included on the back flap of the envelope.

INNER ENVELOPES

Write people's names only, not the address. The inner envelope should read, for example, "Mr. and Mrs. Wilks," without including a first name. If children are invited, their names are written below the parents' names (i.e., Miss Angela Wilks). It is acceptable, with a very close relative, to write a more familiar name on the inner envelope (i.e., Uncle James). If someone has been invited with a date, this would be indicated on the inner envelope, as described above.

WEDDING ANNOUNCEMENTS

Announcements are traditionally worded like a wedding invitation, substituting "announce the marriage" for "request the honour of your company." Announcements should not be mailed prior to the actual wedding.

In a redwood grove
under a blue skye
Cyndi Chambers
and
Dave Crook
will exchange
marriage vows

Please grace us
with your presence

Sunday, June 16, 1
at 1:30 p.m.

Boulder Cr
Scout Reservat
4586 Bear Cree
Boulder Cr

Untiveros & Nathan

Monday, the third of July
two thousand
at three o' clock

Cambridgeport Baptist Church
459 Putnam Avenue, Cambridge, Massachusetts
and afterward at the reception
Le Meridien Hotel, Boston

— I have been te

118 Rosemont Drive
Greenville, South Carolina 29605

Mr. and Mrs. Robert Judson Foste
request the pleasure of your company
at the marriage of their daughter

Barbara Paige
to
Mr. Jason Aeneas Watkins

Saturday, the eleventh of November
Two thousand
o'clock
e Lake
Carolina

Home
th of November
wood Lane
th Carolina

l attend
to attend

Thy people shall be my people   And thy God my God

Where thou d...

Whither thou goest, I will go   And where thou lodgest, I will lodge

Katherine Van Gild...
& John Mich...
Invite you t...
Wes...

You are in...
Rehearsal...
at the home...
Wade & El...
Monday, 3 Ju...
4:00 – 6:00 p....
2125 Broderick...

Mr. and
16 N
G

a gallery of
WEDDING CALLIGRAPHY

Now that you're feeling a little more confident about your calligraphy skills, looking at the work of others can be inspiring. This section of wedding-related art completes the picture—a gallery of the cream of the crop from professional calligraphers. Some of the pieces showcased here raise calligraphy to its highest form. Others are merely exquisite. There is a wonderful assortment of wedding invitation sets, from the uncomplicated to the intricate, and a handful of special projects that directly relate to wedding topics. You'll see the use of inspiring and unusual materials juxtaposed with the elegant simplicity of perfectly executed calligraphy on fine papers. Allow these examples to encourage you and enhance your ideas.

And when the wedding is over, don't pack away your pens. Use your newfound calligraphy skills to write love letters, create anniversary cards, valentines, baby books, and special gifts. Continue to explore and study the extraordinary practice of calligraphy, and you will always find a way to incorporate the art of beautiful writing into your life.

KETUBAH WITH TREE AND ORION

In this magnificent example of an egalitarian ketubah, the couple chose to split the text (which outlines their responsibilities toward one another) into Hebrew and English, rendered in Uncial. A specialty of this artist, the *ketubah* is a legally binding contract of marriage in the Jewish faith. In this piece, the calligrapher began with the watercolor painting, then tackled the lettering using gouache and steel broad-edge nibs.

WEDDING ROUNDEL

Commissioned by the bride as a gift for her groom, this lovely segment from the *Song of Songs* is a classic wedding passage. Lettered in the calligrapher's own modern, Italic hand, the English translation encircles the Hebrew words, all rendered in a style that is as lively and beautiful as the surrounding collage. Both the ketubah on the opposite page and the roundel reflect imagery that is personally meaningful to the couple, translated by the artist's own vision.

MODERN WEDDING SET

This unconventionally stylish set shows how traditional wedding details can be fashionably updated for the forward-looking duo. By including engaging illustrations throughout the pieces, the artist creates a theme for the letterpressed wedding stationery. Invitation and envelope, reception card, response set, program, and thank you notes all tie together in the calligrapher's own unique lettering style, which is simultaneously sweet and hip.

ORNAMENTAL SCROLL WEDDING SET

This incredible scroll crafted on parchment paper has illuminated initial caps highlighting the couple's names. Rich tones of gold and burgundy are a lush counterpoint to the black flourished Italic text. These invitations are usually rolled into a cylinder, tied with a delicate ribbon, and mailed in a coordinating tube, such as the one featured on page 62.

WEDDING BELLS SET

Bringing all his talents to bear, this calligrapher combines his magnificent script with his artistic eye and flair for design in this charming wedding set. Incorporating illustration into a monogram created for the engaged couple, the well-designed pages show just the right amount of embellishment.

HAND-CUT MAT WITH POEM

The Native American wedding blessing shown here in golden Uncial lettering has become a popular reading at many modern ceremonies. The artist cuts each mat by hand. The poem or the shape of the mat can be changed to suit the newlyweds. Combined with a favorite wedding photo, the framed keepsake is an imaginative reminder of the wedding.

TABLE SEATING CHART

Displayed at the reception entrance as an alternative to place cards, this exceptional piece makes a big impression on guests. An increasingly trendy option, the table chart must be carefully planned and executed. Working on a complex chart like this doesn't seem to phase this particular artist, whose beautiful calligraphy and artwork blend harmoniously to make a grand statement.

SNOW-WHITE WEDDING SET

A departure from the often used cream or ecru paper, this pristine wedding set relies on clean design and picture-perfect lettering for its overall, effective loveliness. The full set includes the invitation with outer envelope, reception card, response card, return envelope, and thank you notes, each impeccably rendered in a flourished Italic.

ORGANIC WEDDING SET

The juxtaposition of organic and organza blends beautifully in this eye-catching invitation. Paired with a very fluid Italic, the effect is unique. Reception card, response set, and wedding program all utilize the same flowing lettering style.

WEDDING INVITATION MOTIFS

Two stunning invitations by this calligrapher show how easy it is to match the style of the invitation to the style of the couple and the event. In both of these striking sets, the artist combines a classic Italic lettering style with her inspired renderings to create unique pieces. The invitation of Cyndi Chambers and Dave Crook takes one-of-a-kind to the limit. Each one was hand-printed using the zinc letterpress plate shown here, then wrapped in the bride's handmade green paper.

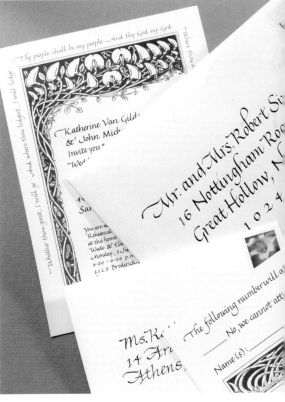

KNOTTED RING WEDDING INVITATION

This unusual package is a perfect example of the artist's ability to marry hand lettering and calligraphy. Each successive sheet of this invitation provides more of the wedding details. The set is tied together with twine and mailed in an envelope written in calligraphic form with his free-flowing characters. For those unable to attend the wedding, the calligrapher created an announcement in a similar style, with a slight variation in the interlocking rings.

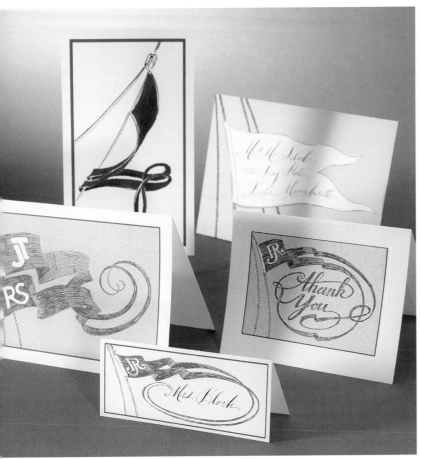

NAUTICAL WEDDING INVITATION

In his signature style, this artist combines graphics and hand lettering with his freestyle script. With a whimsical touch, he transforms the wedding stationery to fit the couple's nautical theme. The front of the invitation is hand lettered with the couple's initials on two flags intertwined in the wind. Ship's flags are used to tie all the pieces together. As shown here, the nautical theme is used throughout—in hand-lettered table numbers, thank you notes, outer envelopes, and place cards.

FENCING WEDDING INVITATION

Touched by love: this couple's interest in fencing is translated into their very personal wedding invitation. Combining typeset text with hand lettering and his sweeping calligraphy, this calligrapher creates a perfect balance in this invitation, which meets in the middle.

ELEGANT WEDDING SET

The rich browns of this artist's inks are not available at your local calligraphy supply shop. She makes her own ink by hand from walnuts to achieve a depth of color that recalls the gentility of days gone by. Perfectly paired with her refined script, lithe flourishes transform into supple stalks of wheat.

MEDIEVAL WEDDING CERTIFICATE

Handcrafted from beginning to end, this impressive scroll is a collaborative effort between husband-and-wife calligraphers to commemorate their own wedding on parchment. Each of their certificates is personalized for its owners using black and gold ink, along with watercolor and gouache to add the "illumination."

RECEPTION TABLE SET

A beautiful menu, escort cards, and table numbers are all expertly fashioned with pointed pen. Graceful flourishes add to the sophisticated elegance of these pieces for the table.

"PAINTED" WEDDING SET

With tongue in cheek, the calligrapher constructed this charming invitation to a painter's wedding. The invitation includes a paintbrush with the couple's names inscribed in delicate script to match the text. It bids guests to help them paint the town. The theme is carried over to the reception, where paintbrushes stand in for place cards.

calligraphy RESOURCES

Association for the Calligraphic Arts
1223 Woodward Avenue
South Bend, IN 46616
Telephone: (219) 233-6233
Fax: (219) 233-6229
http://www.calligraphicarts.org
E-mail: aca@calligraphicarts.org

The Society of Scribes & Illuminators
http://calligraphy.org
E-mail: scribe@calligraphy.org

PUBLICATIONS AND SUPPLIES:
Paper & Ink Arts
calligraphy and art supplies, books, fine papers
3 North Second Street
Woodsboro, MD 21798
Telephone: (800) 736-7772 or (301) 898-7991
Fax: (888) 736-7773
http://www. paperinkarts.com or http://www.paperinkbooks.com
E-mail: paperinkarts@aol.com or paperinkbk@aol.com

John Neal Bookseller
calligraphy and art supplies, books, fine papers, rubber stamp and
embossing supplies
1833 Spring Garden Street
Greensboro, NC 27403
Telephone: 336-272-6139 or 800-369-9598 (Toll free in USA and
Canada)
Fax: (336) 272-9015
http://www.johnnealbooks.com
E-mail: info@johnnealbooks.com

Letter Arts Review
award-winning quarterly magazine for calligraphers and lettering
artists
Post Office Box 9986
Greensboro, NC 27429
Telephone (336) 272-6139 or (800) 348-PENS (Toll free in USA and
Canada)
Fax: (336) 272-9015
http://www.letterarts.com
E-mail: lar@johnnealbooks.com

Ken McCallister's Art Supplies
calligraphy and art supplies, fine papers
500 Salem Avenue
Dayton, OH 45406
Telephone: (937) 278-0844

The Lettering Design Group
calligraphy supplies, videos, books, instruction, and workshops
5830 Nall Avenue
Suite 2
Mission, KS 66202
Telephone: (913) 362-7864
http://www.spencerian.com
E-mail: michael@spencerian.com

Pearl Paint
calligraphy and art supplies, books, fine papers, pressed flowers, rubber
stamp and embossing supplies, frames, mat board
308 Canal Street
New York, NY 10013
Telephone: (212) 431-7932 or (800) 221-6845 x2297 (Toll free)
http://www.pearlpaint.com

Kate's Paperie
fine papers, stationery items, ribbon, handmade paper boxes and
bags, rubber stamp and embossing supplies, pressed flowers
561 Broadway
New York, NY 10012-3918
Telephone: (212) 941-9816
http://www.katespaperie.com
E-mail: info@katespaperie.com

Paper Access
fine papers, stationery and mailing supplies, ribbon, rubber stamp and
embossing supplies, pressed flowers
23 West 18th Street
New York, NY 10011
Telephone: (212) 463-7035 or (800) 727-3701 (Toll free)
Fax: (212) 463-7022 or (800) 813-0908 (Toll free)
http://www.paperaccess.com
E-mail: info@paperaccess.net

A. I. Friedman
calligraphy and art supplies, books, stationery items, fine papers, ribbon, frames, mat board
44 West 18th Street
New York, NY 10011
Telephone: (212) 243-9000
Fax: (212) 242-1238

Sam Flax
calligraphy and art supplies, books, stationery items, fine papers, frames, mat board
12 West 20th Street
New York, NY 10011
Telephone: (212) 620-3038 or (800) 726-3529 (Toll free)
http://www.samflax.com

New York Central Art Supply
calligraphy and art supplies, books, stationery items, fine papers, frames, mat board
62 Third Avenue
New York, NY 10003
Telephone: (212) 473-7705 or (800) 950-6111 (Toll free)
http://nycentralart.com
E-mail: sales@nycentralart.com

Hobby Craft
Stores around the UK
Telephone: 01202 596100
http://www.hobbycraft.co.uk

FONT LIBRARIES:
International Typeface Company
Telephone: (866) 823-5828 (Toll Free)
http://www.itcfonts.com
E-mail: info@itcfonts.com

Linotype Library
http://www.linotypelibrary.com
E-mail: info@fonts.de

Adobe
Telephone: (800) 833-6687 (Toll free in USA and Canada)
http://www.adobe.com

AGFA/Monotype
http://www.agfamonotype.com
E-mail: oem.sales@agfamonotype.com

Brian Hall, Inc.
http://www.calligraphyfonts.com

1001 Free Fonts
http://www.1001freefonts.com

Free Fonts on the Web
http://www.onlinebusiness.com/shops/_computers/BEST_Fonts.shtml

OTHER WEB SITES OF INTEREST
The Calligraphy Ring
http://www.studioarts.net/calligring/index.html

Cynscribe
http://www.cynscribe.com

Alphabytes
http://www.alphabytes.com/calliglinks.html

directory OF ARTISTS

PROJECT CONTRIBUTORS:

Nan DeLuca
New York, NY
Telephone: (212) 477-3732
Fax: (425) 969-8667
http://members.nbci.com/scribenyc/
index.html
E-mail: deluca212@aol.com

Melissa Dinwiddie
Melissa Dinwiddie Designworks
Palo Alto, CA
Telephone: (650) 325-7687
Fax: (650) 325-2615
mddesignworks.com and
melissaink.com
E-mail: info@mddesignworks.com

Lisa J. Kennedy
LJK Calligraphy
Rowley, MA
Telephone: (978) 948-5434
http://www.usabride.com/wed/
calligraphy
E-mail: ljkraffi@gis.net

Bette Matthews
Brooklyn, NY
Telephone/Fax: (718) 857-4699
E-mail: BetteMatthews@aol.com

Susan L. Ramsey
Calligraphic Creations
Norwalk, CT
Telephone/Fax: (203) 847-5715
http://www.callig.com
E-mail: Calligraphic@aol.com

Christopher J. Watkins
Watkins and Watkins Artisans, Inc.
Pickens, SC
Telephone/Fax: 864-878-1357
http://www.watkinsandwatkins.com
E-mail:
watkins-watkins@mindspring.com

Hilary Williams
Hil-Ink Calligraphy
North Hollywood, CA
Telephone: (818) 760-3406
Fax: (818) 760-3912
http://www.hil-ink.com
E-mail: hilary@hil-ink.com

Beverly Wladkowski
B Creative
Ijamsville, MD
Telephone/Fax: (301) 831-6004
http://www.bcreativecalligraphy.com
E-mail: bwladkowski
@bcreativecalligraphy.com

ADDITIONAL GALLERY

CONTRIBUTORS:

Stephannie Barba
Stephannie Barba Calligraphy
San Francisco, CA
Telephone: (415) 437-6001
Fax: (415) 409-0512
E-mail: stephanniebarba@hotmail.com

Sharon D. Eisman
Starr Designs
Warwick, RI
Telephone: (401) 886-9444
Fax: (401) 886-9888
E-mail: StarrDesigns2@aol.com

Cari Ferraro
Prose and Letters
San Jose, CA
Telephone: (408) 293-1852
Fax: (408) 294-7362
http://www.proseandletters.com
E-mail: Cariscribe@aol.com

Pier Gustafson
Somerville, MA
Telephone/Fax: (617) 666-2975
http://members.aol.com/callipg/
index.htm
E-mail: callipg@aol.com

Sally Laporta
Monks of Age
Sunnyvale, CA
Telephone: (408) 296-6665
Fax: (408) 296-6667
http://www.monksofage.com
E-mail: sally@monksofage.com.

Sharon and Steven Schwartz
Calligraphica
Covington, OH
Telephone: (937) 473-2582
http://www.calligraphica.com
E-mail: Ronyer@aol.com

Reubena L. Spence
Spence Calligraphy
Pleasantville, NJ
Telephone: (609) 646-4723
Fax: (609) 272-8775
http://www.inkcurves.com
E-mail: inkcurves@aol.com

Angela R. Welch
Pen and Pauper
Orange Beach, AL
Telephone and Fax: (334) 981-1377
http://www.angelarwelch.com
E-mail: penandpauper@hotmail.com

about THE AUTHOR

Bette Matthews is the author of *The Wedding Workbook, Cakes (For Your Wedding), Wedding Toasts and Vows*, and the upcoming *A Wedding for All Seasons*. She has worked as an event consultant and stylist with a New York caterer, and is in the early stages of a start-up venture designing and producing handmade wedding invitations. Bette lives in New York City with her husband, photographer Antonio M. Rosario, and their two cats.

acknowledgments

Bringing this book to life was a whirlwind of an experience and it has afforded me the opportunity to learn, to grow, and to bond. I must first offer my unending thanks to all the artists who contributed their skills and talents, their effort, and their knowledge to this project. This book was created by them, and because of them, the words have a life of their own. To Sue Ramsey, Melissa Dinwiddie, and Christopher Watkins for their generosity with their expertise and their time, and for their warm hearts and all the extra hand-holding, my particular heartfelt appreciation.

I am indebted to Francine Hornberger, who introduced me to both the idea of this book and to the publisher. My gratitude also goes to the staff at Rockport: Shawna Mullen for the opportunity, Martha Wetherill for getting the ball rolling, Mary Ann Hall for her positive spirit, level-headed patience, and hard work to keep this project on track, and Maryellen Driscoll for her flexibility, late nights, and gentle editor's pen.

To my supportive and understanding husband Antonio, my devotion always, along with my promise to clean up all the pens and ink and paper and ribbon. And my love and appreciation to my father, who introduced me to the world of graphic arts and beautiful letters, and has trusted me with the care and admiration of his wonderful collection of writing tools.